LIAR, LIAR

Praise for *Liar, Liar*

'Rheea writes with wit, warmth and self-awareness about a very specific kind of digital life, one many of us built before we even realized we were building it. For those of us who grew up constructing entire identities online, *Liar, Liar* feels like a living cultural record. The internet may erase traces, but it doesn't erase the emotions, relationships and consequences that lived there.

I came for the gossip—a deliciously messy scam story—but stayed for the deeply empathetic and funny excavation of online social justice, identity and the strange ways the internet shaped who we became.

Equal parts scandalous and thoughtful, this book is unapologetically slutty and intellectual.'

—**Aditi Mittal**, stand-up comedian and actor

'Rheea flexes her strongest muscle here: storytelling. She writes with precision and conviction, bringing out the contradictions and fault lines of left spaces with a rare authenticity that feels both unsettling and unflinching. An easy read that moves and stays with you long after. Rheea Mukherjee really ate with this one.'

—**Aleena S**, writer and poet

'I'm constantly reading for work, and I can't remember the last time I came across something as unputdownable as this book. *Liar, Liar* is an urgent, uncomfortable and fiercely intelligent memoir that remains compulsively readable while refusing spectacle. Rheea Mukherjee writes with unnerving clarity about emotional fraud in this digital age of social justice, crafting a personal account that is devastating, necessary and deeply of our time.'

—**Devrupa Rakshit**, independent journalist

'An honest and unflinching look at our individual and collective vulnerabilities set in the heady and hyper-articulate world of social justice–driven social media. It has the unpredictability of a domestic thriller, peppered with the nuance and self-awareness of critical theory. Delicious!

—**Swara Bhasker**, actor and activist

LIAR, LIAR

THE SCANDALOUS TRUE STORY OF THE SOCIAL JUSTICE SCAMMER WHO FAKED CANCER AND DEATH

RHEEA MUKHERJEE

HARPER
NON-FICTION
An Imprint of HarperCollins *Publishers*

First published in India by Harper Non-Fiction 2026
An imprint of HarperCollins *Publishers*
HarperCollins *Publishers* India, Cyber City,
Building 10-A, Gurugram, Haryana – 122002, India
www.harpercollins.co.in

2 4 6 8 10 9 7 5 3 1

P-ISBN: 978-93-6989-795-7
E-ISBN: 978-93-6989-487-1

Typeset in 11.5 pt/15 Adobe Garamond Pro
by HarperCollins *Publishers* India Pvt. Ltd

Printed and bound in India by
Manipal Technologies Limited

FSC
www.fsc.org
MIX
Paper | Supporting responsible forestry
FSC™ C043100

This book is produced from independently certified FSC® paper to ensure responsible forest management.

HarperCollins *Publishers*, Macken House, 39/40 Mayor Street Upper, Dublin 1, D01 C9W8, Ireland

For Utsav, for holding on, for believing in me, my intentions and my insanity

PRELUDE TO A LIE

'Everything I do not know forms the greater part of me:
This is my largesse. And with this I understand everything.
The things I do not know constitute my truth.'
—Clarice Lispector

This is a consciously lobotomized memoir of my life and how it collided with Sanch. I have surgically removed many people from my story. At the same time, some people and friends are part of this story and have consented to be included in the book, completely trusting how I represent them.

This is not an exposé. It is not a call-out. It is not a reconstruction of Sanch's lies for your consumption. This is a story about what happens to your life, your mind, your self-worth when love becomes a weapon you didn't know was loaded.

My fate as a writer cannot be the fate of others who might be far more impacted and vulnerable than I can afford to be. I know what the aftermath of a public scam can be. I understand how people, even those you thought would have your back, can look at you with pity and distrust. I know how it feels to see people who knew Sanch project their shock into vile, absurd theories about who I am and what my intentions were.

This isn't just a story about being deceived, it's about what betrayal does to your body. It's about what the world does to you when you admit you've been fooled. And it's about the slow, unsexy process of becoming someone who can live with the discomfort of both.

No matter what I write, this book will make folks in her circles uneasy. But I must write. I must write for the people who will inevitably tell their part of the story as time passes. Also, I want to write because I have found more confidence through other writers who gave me the strength to speak up for the different things I believe in. If any human has robbed you of your trust, they think that your vulnerability and fear of all the emotions and parts of you that you shared with them is enough to keep you hostage to them long after they are gone. They make you feel like your regular human flaws are as magnified and scandalous as their pathological narcissism. However, a scam artist cannot rob you of your entire life, your entire person. This book is for anyone who's been shamed into silence because their grief looked inconvenient. For anyone who's been gaslit by not just one person but by the entire social aftermath of that person's actions.

If you've ever been in a similar situation, I want you to know that your freedom to reclaim who you were and who you'll become can start today.

This lobotomized tale is whole. Even if I decided to give you a timeline of each social situation that unravelled Sanch, it would still be my version of events. The truth is more significant than those who may or may not be in this story. The truth, I've discovered, is my ability to stand up and walk after feeling I had to sit in a corner and endure punishment for my stupidity.

So now I walk silly, swaying and clumsy. I walk briskly, almost violently and sometimes gently to reassure the ground beneath me. I walk like a woman who has found her appetite for limitless sovereignty.

The broken fragments of memory and ineffable dimensions of my experience will not prevent me from having the courage to tell you who I am.

I want to be who I am fully, no matter how others cradle this narrative. You may place me on a pedestal, erase me or project your fears on to me. I flinch at the thought but I keep typing.

CHAPTER 1

Let me start with one of a thousand ironies.

I picked up the word 'grifter' from Sanch.

'Marianne is still asking for mutual aid on her stories? She has a fucking iPhone, what a grifter.'

But it was more than mutual aid seekers on Instagram; she used it as a slur to trash any influencer whose opinions she disagreed with. She said it with a calm, blunt confidence I would've never dared to express when I was younger. Back then, she was twenty-six and I was thirty-seven. But my brain's awestruck response to her cool-queer-girl vibe was sixteen and a half.

Sanch had this way of making mockery sound like truth. She'd scroll through Instagram and narrate each post like she was doing a documentary on endangered cringe. She hated hustle culture but loved getting free coffee from people who admired her. She could drag someone for selling recycled activism but also knew exactly how to slip into the right rooms when it suited her.

I didn't clock it back then. I just thought she was complicated. And I thought complicated meant honest.

And maybe a part of me just wanted to be like her. I had spent my teens and twenties stuffed into the role of the agreeable girl, the one who carefully edited her opinions in real time, who rehearsed how not to make people uncomfortable. I wanted to be someone who could say 'grifter' out loud without flinching. Someone who didn't have to clean up their sentences or soften their edges to be allowed in.

This will all sound foolish in retrospect. There are parts of this story where you, as an outsider, will scrunch your forehead and whisper, *Wait, did you not see that?* Moments that might trigger secondhand embarrassment. Others that may stir justified irritation, anger or even shame.

But it could still happen to you. Not in the same way, not with the same people, but in some shape or form, it could. Of that, I am sure.

It could be a person on the internet who catches you at your loneliest hour and tells you you're beautiful, extraordinary, unlike anyone else. Months later, you find yourself sending them gifts, money, bits of yourself you didn't mean to offer. It might be a friend of a friend who generously compliments your untapped 'business genius' and, before you can taste the fine print, you've sunk money into her idea. This shiny thing eventually leaves you in debt. It could be a mentor who spots your potential but gives you just enough praise to keep you circling, hungry for more.

It could be an ex who resurfaces just when your heart is softest, knowing exactly which memories to unearth. It could even be a sibling or a best friend who has made a quiet career of making you feel small, their behaviour subtle enough to keep you forever chasing their validation.

Sometimes the con isn't spectacular. Sometimes it's just the ordinary cruelties we grow used to. The slow drip of small manipulations we mistake for love.

That, too, is an emotional scam. One that can run decades without anyone calling it what it is.

I'm not writing this as a public warning. A Sanch isn't something you can predict. Not someone you can prepare for. A Sanch is someone you only start to understand once you've reckoned with yourself, who you were, what you wanted and what you were willing to overlook to feel whole.

An emotional scam is an autopsy of the heart—what it desired, what it latched on to and what it was left with to stitch back together.

I met Sanch on Instagram. I can only be as honest as memory allows. Her old Instagram accounts, our early conversations: deleted, deactivated, discarded into the digital ether.

Weeks after the scam had been called out, I kept scrolling, looking for her. But all I ever found was myself, staring back, a little less sure of who I was. The truth is, even after the body is buried, the ghost keeps typing, the scam isn't over. It has just gone silent.

Sometimes I have to research my own past just to be reminded of it. It's the start of 2025 as I write this and I've forgotten how much purpose and chaos I lived through just a few years ago.

For instance, my friend Nisha and I, along with a few others, figured out a system to get groceries into the hands of those with zero access to wages during the COVID-19 outbreak and lockdown.

Between April 2020 and June 2021, we raised ₹24 lakh in pledges for ration kits, mostly in Bangalore. The model worked because it was transparent. We'd post calls on Facebook and Instagram, asking people to pledge. Each kit cost ₹1,000 and included lentils, oil, rice, salt, masalas, soap and sometimes vegetables, enough to feed a family of three or four for two weeks.

Nisha and I coordinated with local shopkeepers who prepared and bagged the kits. We'd call pledgers, ask them to pay the grocer directly via GPay or UPI, then pass the bags to volunteers and citizen welfare workers.

By mid-2021, we were consistent enough to attract media attention. We urged others to replicate the model in their own cities. All you needed was a shopkeeper, a list of pledgers and a rough map of neighbourhoods hardest hit by the lockdown. And, to their credit, the police never interfered with our unofficial aid work, even in the middle of curfews and chaos.

Some moments remain etched in my mind—bright, strange islands in the coma of endless days. The COVID paranoia. The surreal experience of being semi-trapped at home for over a year. At the time, community work probably saved me from a full mental breakdown. I've always been restless. Most of my adult life has been lived under the weight of chronic depression and undiluted self-esteem issues. The project gave me a sliver of peace. A strange calm while the world outside was unravelling.

And yet, in retrospect, the deceit of narrative is this: amplify one part of your life and it can blot out all the other startling, life-changing things happening alongside it.

I don't say this to sound boastful, but my personal life hasn't been average. It's the result of a chaotic, itinerant youth and massively good-hearted intentions. I can't squeeze the absurdity and wildly entertaining anecdotes of forty-one years into one book. But I want to. I want to look at everything that happened with Sanch through the lens of my larger, messier life.

You might wonder why a thirty-seven-year-old woman was so awestruck by Sanch. I have some vague observations about my life that can offer some insight.

My entire adulthood has been a series of mini-lives. I rarely knew when one ended and another began. But every five years or so, I demolished and rebuilt.

My first genuinely indefensible decision was dropping out of college at the age of twenty to get married.

I spent the first ten years of my life in the US, the next eight in Bangalore, India. Why? Don't ask. Not yet. Just as I was starting to feel at home in Bangalore, finally passing my PUC (pre-university) and falling in love with my street theatre group, my family decided to pack up and move back to the US. This time, they picked a state by throwing darts (okay, fingers) at a map: Colorado.

Many of you may have been children in 2002. I was eighteen, being shipped back to America with my family to restart life in the primarily white and admittedly beautiful city of Denver.

Two months later, I moved to Fort Collins, a college town two hours north. My parents stayed in Denver to reactivate their careers, my father as a real-estate agent and my mother as a registered nurse.

I was now an Indian American kid majoring in social work at a state college. I immediately switched back to my American accent, a third-culture-kid party trick, to blend in with my new roommates. They were mostly white, mostly diagnosed and shockingly open about it. Their offhand remarks about anxiety meds and therapy appointments left me uneasy. I hadn't even begun to excavate my demons, let alone discuss them over plastic trays of scrambled eggs and cantaloupe in the dorm cafeteria.

But I adapted. The ruthless rigour of Indian academics made college here feel almost leisurely. My grades reflected that. Then came the parties: sticky shots of cinnamon whisky and coconut rum, the soundtrack of my dorm set to the explicit poetry of Khia's 'My Neck, My Back'.

The white girls would sway, pre-twerk era, mouthing lyrics that made my heart stop mid-beat:

My neck, my back
Lick my pussy and my crack …
Lick it good, suck this pussy just like you should

I'd stand there and watch them casually take off their shirts and pyjamas, dancing in their underwear. And when I say underwear, I mean thongs, because almost every eighteen-year-old woman in 2003 America wore them. I'd stand in the corner and dance, fully clothed, wanting to understand what that kind of security in sexuality felt like.

It's not like Indian college girls didn't have our moments. In pre-university, we talked about sex, made out with boys in the corners of movie theatres and giggled about the stupidest shit while splitting a dosa at the Darshini next to school.

But this was different. My dorm friends' freedom with their bodies, their unashamed sexuality, clashed with their naivety about the larger world. It confused me.

Sometimes, boys came with their ubiquitous hats, T-shirts and long shorts and asked me questions like, 'Do you speak Hindu?' or 'Do you have planes in India?' I answered politely but with smugness. For the first time in my life, I felt exceedingly intelligent. Indian schooling had extracted every cell of self-esteem out of me, but it had taught me things these Americans didn't know.

Still, I longed to feel as unbridled, unabashed and good-looking as them. I drank alcohol for the first time in a dorm room; my roommate, the kindest of them all, told me to stop after five back-to-back shots of cinnamon liquor. I spent the whole night vomiting into the shared bathroom pot, regurgitating a putrefied, sickly-sweet cinnamon, thick and syrupy in a way it absolutely was not while drinking.

By the end of my first semester, I had tasted all there was to the American college experience. It was just another coat of paint layered over the fragments of my identity. I was a child of sexual abuse. I had failed the Indian schooling system. I was a teenager in love with Bollywood. I had no fucking clue who I was.

At eighteen, I had escaped the contradictions and emotional vacancy of my parents. Indian parents often offer relationships that are both overbearing and emotionally absent. It includes deep paranoia about your safety, paired with a startling inability to ask how you're really doing.

Finally, I had some independence. That was cool. But I loathed how Americans treated me.

'Are you Indian American or just an FOB [fresh off the boat]?' they asked.

I was both. And I could barely explain that to myself.

I wanted to stuff my face with pancakes and run like the white girls in super-short shorts through the midwinter campus. I wanted to be the bright, exotic brown girl in my psych class. I wanted my hips to not stick out. I wanted my legs to be long and lean like my roommates'. I wanted to be loved, desired, cherished.

But I was also homesick for India, for Bangalore. My friends and our theatre group back home felt wildly intelligent, even though most had never left India. 'These Americans don't even know Sri Lanka is a country,' I'd laugh on the phone with friends back home. In those moments, I felt manically magical.

So, I distanced myself from the dorm kids and joined the hippies protesting George Bush's war in Iraq, a tiny minority who danced in circles around campus, chanting: 'There ain't no power like the power of the people!'

Their beaded dreadlocks swung in rhythm with their drums. But even they felt far from my world.

I wanted to protest war *and* talk about *DDLJ*, Bipasha Basu and the songs in *Devdas*. So, I joined the Indian Students Association at Colorado State University. Of course I did. Our need to invent or locate identities to feel whole—that need is a risk. A vulnerability. A social manipulation waiting to happen.

Because a scam is rarely just about money. It's about emotional pressure points. The places we reach for when we're desperate. We ask them to save us and we know they won't but we need the relief anyway.

I met a man at the Indian Students Association. He was doing his master's. Conservative. Your typical cishet North Indian boy who sang me all the Bollywood I wanted. Damn, it was a sweet, sweet relief.

It was the beginning of a cycle. One that would repeat in unexpected forms. One that would root itself in patterns I wouldn't fully recognize until much later.

Patterns that, seventeen years later, would lead me straight to Sanch.

~

So much happened in 2021 beyond the community work. That year, Write Leela Write, the content and design lab I cofounded in 2014, shut down due to the pandemic. I got married again at a sub-registrar's office in J.P. Nagar to my partner, Utsav, whom I'd met on Bumble just the year before.

Later that year, I got my first corporate job, at a Singaporean brand consultancy, after over a decade of rejecting anything that resembled a nine to five. Until then, my career had been stitched together from social work in the US, grad school in California and then writing workshops and creative communications as an entrepreneur back in India.

And yes, it was also the year I met Sanch.

Our first interaction was on Instagram. I can only approximate the time, maybe April 2021. I'd shared a post about someone in Assam seeking mutual aid for a few transwomen and an online acquaintance asked if anyone could redirect pledges. That's when I DMed Sanch to ask her for more details about the women she was trying to help.

Sanch responded. She said she was helping transwomen in her hometown of Silchar, Assam, who urgently needed medicine. She sent me a doctor's prescription and medical bills. I told her it was wonderful she was helping and I'd check with pledgers to see who could cover it.

Most pledgers were generous, happy to help wherever they could. I quickly found a few willing to pay the medical shop directly. Sanch thanked me for handling the logistics.

Good intent, however pure, is always brushed with the itch of pride. The saviour in me inflated. It felt good, like something I'd built in Bangalore could stretch all the way to Assam, a town I hadn't even heard of before.

That first interaction faded into the chaos of that year. But Sanch stayed on my radar.

She stood out.

Her Instagram presence started to coat my brain and heart.

She was the person I had wanted to be in my twenties—sharp, brash, politically clear. She had the right opinions and the context to back them. She wasn't afraid to talk about her body, her desires or her critiques of mainland Indian perspectives on the Northeast. She wasn't afraid to talk about her mental illnesses either, captioned and layered right on top of semi-naked selfies in her stories.

I was fascinated.

And I was about to be consumed.

I've been wildly jealous and deeply grateful that Instagram didn't exist when I was in my twenties. As a geriatric millennial, I have one foot in the analogue world and the other in digital. We romanticize a time without smartphones, yet we've adapted to Instagram therapy, tweets and selfies like they were always parts of us. No generation has normalized a technological transition quite like ours.

Still, I envy them: the twenty-somethings of the 2020s. There's a low hum of resentment as I watch a generation claim autonomy through the glitter and grit of social media. They unlearn faster. They are fluent in naming relational toxicity and oppressive systems. They talk about mental health, queerness and the failures of Indian schooling with a confidence I had to claw my way towards. They have the language, the articulation, the emojis. They learned the dialect of liberation long before we did.

I wrote obsessively on Facebook before it died. If you scrolled through my old posts, you might think I was confident: ranting about politics, gender and oppression, softened with the occasional vegan pasta recipe. But inside, I was a toddler. Wide-eyed. Absorbing the petty e-lafdas and the exhilarating moments of intellectual kinship I found with other writers.

Middle-class Gen X-adjacent millennials carry the baggage of intelligence measured in tweed jackets and ceramic teacups. To be intellectual was to be calm, restrained, appropriately posed. Saying 'fuck', being casual, laughing at yourself—those were unserious, even obnoxious. But I secretly loved it. I wanted to be brash. I wanted to shred the performance of being well-read in the 'right' way.

What I didn't realize then was that much of what I was trying to emulate, what confused and alienated me, was just savarna culture dressed up as intellect.

And then came Gen Z, smashing the rules.

If you were paying attention, you saw it. I certainly did.

I read their posts: unapologetic, relentless. They spoke of queerness, anti-caste history, trauma and politics not like academics but like prophets. My closest brush with confidence had been authority: the bark of Indian schooling. No matter how 'liberal' our urban lives were, we were still choking on gender roles and the rigid expectations of 'good' Indian values.

No one embodied that generational shift like Sanch. Brazen. Unfiltered. Opinionated to the point of detachment. Many found her off-putting, her truths delivered without softness or social grace.

But in my DMs, she was warm. She got it. She made me feel like I was beyond critique.

Part of it was me—I played the student. I rarely brought the full weight of my own wisdom into our conversations. I held it back, kept it folded. Maybe I wanted her to feel unthreatened. Maybe I wanted her to like me. When I asked her questions, she answered them like I was one of the good ones. 'Yeah, you're not like the asshole wokes. You're different,' she'd say. It wasn't loud praise, it was the quiet kind, the kind that sinks in and stays there. The kind that makes you want to keep proving it's true.

And I violated my own rule.

Theory without compassion is hollow. I had no real tangible evidence of her actual compassion except for her words that indicated it.

What made her warmth feel so singular? Maybe because it wasn't saccharine. It was sharp. Fast. Delivered with the precision of someone who knows exactly which nerve to press. I didn't want coddling; I wanted to be seen without performance. No one else was offering that. Everyone else needed context, disclaimers, carefulness. Sanch didn't. She offered affirmation like it was currency she printed herself. I didn't realize yet that it was a seduction strategy, the way some people weaponize insight to make you feel uniquely understood. And I lapped it up. Not because I was naive. But because I was starving. And she had studied hunger.

At the time, it didn't matter.

I wanted Sanch to pick me.

Pick me, Sanch. I want to be as blunt, as extraordinary as you. Pick me, I'm the late-thirty-something-year-old who gets it.

Can a friendship be built on the shrapnel of social media identities?

Social media doesn't smell. It doesn't flinch. It doesn't reveal hesitation. You curate your best angles, your sharpest wit, your causes, your coffee. But Gen Z taught us that even our worst days, our bedridden, stained, depressive selves, could be curated and consumed.

You could post a picture of yourself in existential despair, followed by a hot-pink-lipped selfie. Cropped just right. Filtered just enough. It's beautiful to suffer and resist oppression online.

So how do these curations shape friendship?

It's lazy to say social media is fake. That refrain's gone stale. These friendships are real. Just like traditional ones, they can be shallow or profound. What matters is how they mutate. Some fade. Some grow roots. Some show up out of nowhere and stay longer than you ever imagined.

Within weeks, I knew more about Sanch than I probably should have. She posted most of it on her stories. All I had to do was ask.

Her father was dying. Cancer. Her mother had died in a car accident when she was sixteen. She couldn't sit in the back seat of a car without anxiety gripping her chest. At twenty-six, she had carried more than most.

I carried her trauma in my brain.

My life, by contrast, wasn't dramatic on paper. Atypical, sure. But not tragic. I was born in the US, spent my first ten years there, then moved to Bangalore in the '90s. My teenage years? A shit show. Trauma. Sexual abuse. Academic failure. Mocked for being too American, too fat, too stupid.

But no one died. My parents provided everything materially. Emotionally, I had no room to exist as myself. I mimicked accents, food preferences, mannerisms. I had a personality but it never felt safe enough to emerge.

Indians don't value confidence in women unless it's cloaked in 'good studies' and ladylike silence. A good girl doesn't swear. Doesn't resist too hard. Doesn't ruin her reputation.

That's the hallmark of any Brahminical-savarna upper-middle-class upbringing—even in a mixed marriage like my parents'. A Catholic Mangalorean mother. A Hindu Bengali father. Caste and class whispered through everything, my confusion, my privilege, my despair. The most insidious part? You can live your whole life and never see it.

But Sanch broke that for me.

She was part of the rising Gen Z on Instagram: the rebels, the anti-caste feminists, the political influencers who wore their inherited shame like armour and lobbed sharp truth bombs with it. I fell for that world. It was electric. It was liberating.

And the dark underbelly?

That could've broken me.

Remember those American roommates I told you about? The ones who were already diagnosed and talking about therapy in the dorm cafeteria? That dissonance stuck with me.

By 2005, I was working in a domestic violence shelter as part of my social work degree. My first full-time job was as a residential behavioural counsellor in a step-down-from-jail facility for boys aged eleven to nineteen. Kids pulverized by the system and by their families: vandalism, drug peddling, abuse. I wanted to save them. To help. To be the emotional healer I'd never had.

In retrospect, I wasn't just saving them. I was trying to save myself.

By my early twenties, I was already on Zoloft. My parents were skittish. But this was still a time when mental illness wasn't romanticized. No five million memes. No TikToks about bed rot. No Instagram story templates diagnosing your abandonment wounds.

We didn't even know complex post-traumatic stress disorder (CPTSD) existed or that nearly every close friend I would make as an adult would be carrying it.

By thirty, I had stopped whispering. I broke all the rules. I wrote about depression, oppression, hierarchy, my body, things I wouldn't have dared to say out loud in my twenties.

Honestly, my twenties were a past life.

By the time Sanch entered the picture, I had already shocked myself with what I'd survived and built.

In 2019, my debut novel was published. It got reviewed in the *LA Times*. I taught classes. Sat on panels. Ran my own business.

I was a stranger to the discombobulated, emotionally unregulated, double-divorcée child I'd been in my twenties.

By then, I was fluent in the dialect of mental health. I knew the terms, the diagnoses, the critiques: for and against pharma, meds, therapy, Insta-therapy and all the godforsaken discourse that came with it.

The one thing I hadn't faced? A full diagnosis. Of what was really wrong with me.

I floated from doctor to doctor, just before they could figure it out. No matter how neatly the *Diagnostic and Statistical Manual of Mental Disorders* (DSM) tried to label it, no single box ever fully applied. I'd always just had classic depression: non-spicy, chronic, aching and sometimes intolerable.

Until one day, months after Sanch had left my life in shambles, I ended up with a nervous breakdown. Or as I called it, my MentyB.

The doctor listened to fragments of my story and then mumbled, 'Maybe we should test you for something more ... some personality issue ...'

She lowered her voice. I visibly flinched.

No. Not the personality disorder stuff. Please, not that.

See, I had rage.

And personality disorders never made sense to me except, maybe, one: antisocial personality disorder.

That's the one I'd throw at Sanch.

I wanted to stamp the label across her forehead like a scarlet letter: ANTISOCIAL PERSONALITY. But I only let myself feel that way when I made space for the rage she left behind.

I often wonder how many Sanches are out there. How many lie like they breathe. How many live entire lives stitched together from pity and performance.

Most people never truly understand their own personality, buried as it is under the weight of roles, rules and rituals. You're lucky if any authentic part of you survives orthodox schooling, gender norms, caste scripts or the relentless performance of being a 'good' person.

So, what even is a personality disorder?

Sometimes I think the disorder is the world itself. A place designed to stamp out authenticity.

What makes you *you* once you peel back the weight of expectation and conditioning?

Fuck if I know.

Sanch was bright. Like, *legit.* She regularly posted about the micropolitics of Assam, especially the marginalization of tea tribes and Bengali Muslims. She wrote long, informed burns designed to sting 'mainlanders', as she called the rest of us.

Of course I had to be better than the average mainlander. I was a bougie Bangalorean with an American accent. My biggest insecurity? That I would be seen as just another yoga-class-attending, oat-latte-sipping savarna bimbo.

So, I asked questions. And Sanch answered.

She taught me about the Barak Valley movement. In 1960, eleven ethnic Bengalis were killed by Assam police during protests in Silchar. Even though the region had a

Bengali-speaking majority and multiple tribes, the Assam government had tried to enforce Assamese as the sole official language. In 1961, a series of protests, violence and a public reckoning led to Bengali being reinstated as an administrative language.

We never learned this in Indian schools.

Our textbooks told us Dr Ambedkar wrote the Constitution. But only in my thirties did I actually read him and witness the searing, revolutionary brilliance of his work.

These were the things Sanch could talk about effortlessly. At twenty-six, she seemed to know every revolutionary worth quoting and all the nuance behind them.

Or maybe she just googled a new topic each week, hyper-focused on it and turned it into a carousel post.

Honestly, that might have been it.

It's funny. When I wrote my first novel, *The Body Myth*, I knew so much about French existentialism because my character was obsessed with it. Today, I can't remember a quarter of what I had read or watched. I had hyper-focused, just to make sure the character didn't sound fake.

Now I wonder: do regular people do that much research just to *be* a version of themselves?

Maybe. But that's not the trick.

Ingesting information is one thing. Distilling it? Massaging it into social-justice poetry?

That takes a certain cunning.

And that's what I find hard to grasp, that someone could be *that* smart, *that* articulate and have not one drop of actual feeling.

It was all just a net of beautiful words cast at an audience.

And I?

I was her target audience.

Sanch told me that mental illness was a bitch. That she'd write books, too, if she weren't so sick. I encouraged her. I was sick too. But I'd written books.

I decided her illness was bigger. Worse. Less explainable.

More importantly, I wasn't an Adivasi-Dalit orphan living in a small town in Assam. And that's when the broken child in me stirred.

She woke up, rubbed her sleepy eyes in my adult body and got to work.

The saviour's heart beat harder.

I had to help Sanch become the best version of herself.

She deserved it. She deserved *me* at my best.

Fuck.

CHAPTER 2

Sanch is good-looking.

You can be as self-aware as you want but let's not pretend: people who look and speak a certain way get treated better. She has cherubic cheeks, a neutral, aspirational Indian English accent and a broad, disarming smile. She is fair-skinned. And she knew how to wield it.

She is also witty, righteous and fluent in the vocabulary of justice. She defended trans rights, sex workers, marginalized castes and animals with the kind of conviction that made people stop scrolling.

And then there is her tragedy. Her life was already a slow-burning heartbreak. That's the uncomfortable part to admit, how tragedy gets filtered through palatability. We're more likely to want to save someone if they meet certain metrics. Do they look a certain way? Speak a certain way? Present with just enough vulnerability to feel noble but not so much it makes us squirm? Sanch hit all those notes.

Social-justice Instagram is obsessed with deconstructing oppression like peeling an onion: remove the layers to reveal class, caste, colour, fatphobia, disability, chronic illness, mental health. But in practice, we still engage primarily with our class peers. The rest? The delivery person. The domestic worker. The auto driver.

Even within our class, hierarchy thrives. Who speaks polished English? Who looks good while protesting? Who tweets the right take first? That's why genocides happen with barely a murmur, why white school shooters aren't terrorists, just 'troubled'. Why an upper-caste woman's rape floods headlines while a Dalit woman's barely gets a whisper.

Aesthetics, tone, class signalling: it's all coded into our empathy. It's shrunk. We've become fluent in the choreography of oppression but clumsy at the actual business of feeling it. bell hooks told us love is nothing without practice, but we've settled for performative tenderness, the kind that photographs well. Susan Sontag reminded us that seeing suffering does not guarantee an ethical response, that attention can slide into consumption. Kancha Ilaiah Shepherd pulled the tablecloth off polite tables where caste slips in, uninvited but always seated. Gail Omvedt mapped revolutions as lived, breathing struggles—work that has since reached newer, previously uninitiated audiences, even as it is thinned out, softened, and made legible through the language of shares, captions and comfort. We've grown articulate in the ways of pain but, somewhere along the way, forgotten how to sit with grief without turning it into an accessory. Every day is either a self-flagellation of privilege or performative outrage. No one's got time for complexity. No one's got patience for repair.

'That's what upper castes are like, I guess. Only their oppression is relevant.'

Sanch had texted me that in June 2023 while defending a friend from a marginalized caste. I agreed with her. But these conversations with Sanch weren't surface-level. Not in the circles we swam in. These were the kinds of conversations that demanded you flay your ego, unlearn your schooling and question your place in every room you enter.

We were both animal-rights advocates. Vegans. Sanch and a few other anti-caste vegans (a tiny faction of an already small minority in India) had a lot to say—sharp, needed stuff—about rejecting white/savarna veganism while still maintaining that nuance, caste analysis and structural critique mattered. They weren't trying to win mainstream approval. They were trying to build an ethic that felt lived.

The problem? Nobody likes vegan propaganda. I've always hated the standard playbook—the depoliticized, shame-bait, crying-cow videos served up as moral superiority. The mainstream vegan narrative is whitewashed, weepy and wildly disconnected from systemic violence. This is because it conveniently erases the people who actually touch animals for a living—migrant workers, Dalit labourers, people in slaughterhouses—whose exploitation runs parallel to the animals they kill. It preaches abstinence from meat without touching corporate supply chains, caste-based labour or food insecurity. It screams about animal cruelty but stays politely silent about indigenous food practices, subsistence hunting or the global south's complicated relationship with survival and diet. It's a narrative that demands purity but only from the margins. It forgives the Nature's Basket shopper but shames the working-class eater.

But animal rights have always mattered deeply to me and to many anti-caste activists who recognize how speciesism intersects with caste and labour and how we dehumanize entire groups. Sanch *got* that. She could argue it down to the bone. She had the receipts, the citations, the moral clarity. She'd point out how savarnas loved to show 'solidarity' with Dalit people by eating meat—it was such a convenient, Instagrammable rebellion—but rarely would they trace the actual labour behind the leather industry, the caste lines that tether those who clean, who skin, who scrape. She'd peel it back further, showing how even within humanity we fracture ourselves, as if we were separate species, rejecting those we consider lowly, ugly, disabled, weird.

If we can do that to each other, she'd ask, is it so surprising we do it to animals? Isn't it, in fact, the same fight?

At the same time, she'd roast PETA without mercy. She once laughed at one of their ads and said: 'Look at this nonsense, don't eat red meat or you'll get erectile dysfunction, as if the moral crisis here is about your limp dick.' Even animal rights campaigns, she'd argue, have to pander to health fears and fragile egos to get humans to care. We'll never get anywhere like that.

Unless you are one of those WHATEVER, I'M EATING BACON RIGHT NOW reactionaries, you would not be walking out of those debates feeling smart.

In July 2023, Sanch visited me in Bangalore. It would be her second and last visit to my house. She had flown in from Hyderabad.

Back then, there were parts of her life that never quite added up but I told myself to file them under 'not my business'. For example, she often made mysterious trips to Delhi, citing college applications or visits to friends. The college bit never fully tracked. She already had a political science degree from Jadavpur University. But after her father died, she said she wanted to start from scratch, study psychology, get a new undergraduate degree.

In 2023, she moved to Hyderabad to enrol. A few months in, she claimed the college didn't offer an honours programme and that she'd have to look into options in Delhi. I remember thinking: Isn't that something you'd check before moving across the country? But Sanch had this cold, clipped energy when you asked specific questions. The kind of tone that made you feel like you were overstepping. And maybe I was, maybe I wasn't. But with her, the line was always conveniently blurred. I brushed it off as insecurity. Confusion. A young woman navigating her path without parents or money. That made sense to me.

The thing was, Sanch could be razor-sharp about other things. Her memory, her research and her opinions were always delivered with unnerving specificity. So, the lack of clarity here should've been a red flag. But that's hindsight. Back then, her precision was her credibility. When someone can tell you, in vivid detail, about a small town in Assam, about a particular tea tribe, about how they exacted revenge on their landowners, it doesn't occur to you to cross-examine them.

One story stuck with me. She described a landowner who adored his dog, fed him three hearty meals a day and treated him better than the people who worked his land. One day, while the landowner was away, a man from the tribe poisoned the dog. Not for survival. Not for some strategic gain. Simply to witness grief on the face of a man who believed he could exploit humans but keep one creature safely in his affections.

It's the kind of story that sits in your gut the wrong way. Why did the dog have to die? But Sanch would make a case for it. This, too, she'd argue, was resistance. She'd admit she felt bad for the dog but insisted the point stood.

At the time, I felt rattled yet oddly convinced. I didn't push. I wanted to believe her. I tried to think that someone who could tell stories with this much precision was probably telling the truth about everything else, too. The specifics didn't invite more questions. The specifics *were* the facts. And that was how the gaps stayed hidden.

I used to think most people who were out to get you were looking for money. But with Sanch, the money was never for her. Every ask was framed as a donation for 'the public', often something as mundane as buying supplies directly off Amazon. She never hinted at wanting more from me, never pushed for anything odd or indulgent. She didn't need to. She was—unfortunately—far too smart for a clumsy grab. She wasn't running a quick con. She was playing the long game.

Sanch's queerness tended to be proclaimed in confusing ways. She definitely bragged about loving and dating women. Pussy is what she liked—or, at least, that's what she said. But then there would come more complex stories about her sexual history, as I'd slowly find out.

Sanch's money situation was also very mysterious. After her father died during the pandemic, she had a family home to bank on. But there was more. She would get her father's life insurance at some point, allowing her to be financially secure for the foreseeable future. But before she got it, she was, for all practical purposes, poor, resorting to small gigs that never lasted more than a month. She always blamed it on toxic corporate culture or a toxic boss. I, the ever-generous friend, would offer to pay for her cab fare to and from the airport and my house. I'd buy her coffee at cafes and dinners. I'd send money to her friend's animal rescue farm in Assam whenever needed.

I had structure. I was thirty-seven, a published author with a long streak of entrepreneurial hustles and, at the time, I was working a full-time job. My partner, Utsav, and I were DINKs (Double Income, No Kids). It meant we had extra money. I spent mine being the generous friend. The one who picks up the tab, stocks the guest room, checks in.

But Sanch never asked for money. That's the thing. She didn't have to. When I asked if she was struggling, she'd say things like, 'My life is so fucked but I'm independent. I've done cam work to get by, I have my ways.'

She wore her financial chaos like a badge: she was feral, self-sufficient, too proud to ever beg. If anything, she was the one constantly raising money for animal rescues, for trans kids cut off from their families. That only made me want to give her more. Trust her more. Help her more.

On her last trip to my home, things felt easy. We walked to cafes. She hung out at home while I went to work. I'd call to check if she'd eaten. One day, she made pani puri for everyone and we stood around the table crunching spicy, potato-filled puris, laughing about how pathetic Bangalore pani puri was.

Everything seemed chill, except she was a little jumpy. If I walked into the room and said her name, she'd freeze for a few seconds, then exhale like she'd just dodged a bullet. 'Sorry, BPD [borderline personality disorder],' she'd say. 'Always on edge.'

Fair. I was just a depressive with moderate attention deficit disorder (ADD). Who was I to judge someone for flinching when I called their name?

That same trip, we made what I thought symbolized the peak of our friendship: an epic Instagram reel. It was witty, sharp and delightfully offensive, a parody about meat-eating hypocrisy and animal rescue culture.

The setup? We were regional chefs preparing a dish called cat biryani. It starred my cat, Dua. In the video, we held her lovingly, explaining how fresh meat was key. Then we 'cut away' for the unpleasant parts, returning with a pot of paper scraps labelled 'cat legs', 'eyes', 'ears'. We stirred them with spices.

The punchline? Us devouring a bowl of pulav while Sanch deadpanned, 'If you liked this video, donate to my dog rescue that helps marginalized dogs.'

It was savage. It was smart. People loved it.

For me, it wasn't just a fun moment; it was something more profound. Our dark-humoured, politically irreverent minds had synced. This was the kind of creative mischief I'd always wanted to make. The version of me I wanted at all times—fully expressed, unapologetically weird, sharp and loud—was finally showing up.

But it didn't last long. Sanch returned to Assam to visit her extended family in Silchar. She got dengue just days after leaving and asked me to send her memes to cheer her up. She whined about the fever draining her strength but she did it with her characteristic charismatic glee, making illness sound almost playful.

And then, there was stillness.

A few quiet days. No texts. No memes. No punchy one-liners.

A stillness I didn't recognize.

Not yet.

CHAPTER 3

My body interpreted Sanch as a threat far before my mind could. There was a familiar glitch in my system, an electric zap I felt on a cellular level when I was around her. It temporarily shut off parts of what my brain was telling me.

I still have trouble trusting my body and its extraordinary capacity to inform of threats. It was much worse when I was younger though. When I was a child struggling with multiple traumas and adaptations, significant geographical shifts, sexual abuse by a driver and an art teacher and my absolute inability to deal with school, being in a frozen state had become my natural way to cope. Inside, I was frozen; my head could think, imagine and question so much but my body would not comply; it would not allow my mind, personality and essence to be activated. Sanch was a regression to that early state. She held the same confidence and authority I could never question in my childhood.

For that era of my life, Sanch was an alarming contradiction. In all other areas, I was able to poke holes and illustrate how authority disguises nasty levels of power and manipulation. Sanch wasn't an authority figure to me but, for unknown reasons, my body treated her as such.

I spent time with Sanch in person on two occasions, during her visits to Bangalore. Each time, she stayed at my home as a guest, at my invitation. The first visit was in October 2022 and the second was the last time I saw her, in July 2023.

After a year of our friendship blooming online, Sanch texted to say she could finally visit me in Bangalore. She was going to Mumbai to meet some friends and had found cheap tickets to Bangalore from there. I was super excited but also nervous.

Sanch stood outside my door at 4 a.m. on the last morning of October 2022. I woke up suddenly from the sound of the doorbell; I had tried to stay awake but had fallen asleep at some point. Utsav grumbled about the noise but immediately fell back asleep. I threw off the sheets and rushed downstairs. Jeera, my Indie brindle dog, ran down with me, howling as I fumbled with the door, my eyes only half-open. Sanch was dressed casually in loose pyjama-like pants and an oversized T-shirt. She looked charming, just as she appeared in her online photos, without the glamour of her lipstick-filled selfies. Instead, she had a goofy, perhaps hesitant, grin on her face as she stood there clutching the telescopic handle of her large suitcase.

'Good morning,' she said with a giggle.

As someone nearly forty years old inviting a twenty-something-year-old to my house, I had set clear boundaries beforehand. I had told her I wasn't a drinker, didn't stay out late and had work during the day. I intended my role to be similar to that of a cautious older sister. Sanch, being playful, would jokingly call me 'Auntie'. I embraced this by framing all my boundaries light-heartedly, describing them as 'auntie stuff'. It was an easy, self-deprecating way to convey my message without sounding too much like an actual auntie.

Now, I generously smiled and hugged her as if she were a long-lost sibling. From the corner of my eye, I caught her cautiously inspecting Jeera, who was a jumbled mess, barking, wagging tail and sniffing around her feet. As sleepy as I was in those few seconds, my body recorded a minor inconsistency. A barely-there, subtle form of contradiction that came from relationality. That knowledge you gather through familiarity with shared cultures and specific practices. I'd liken this to a nurse who knows a patient has a slight fever before touching them or taking their temperature, like the tender-coconut seller who knows which coconut has only water and no flesh.

Sanch loved animals. She posted plenty of pictures of cats in her house in Assam, including a skinny rescue called Millie that featured on her posts for a while. She fed stray dogs wherever she could. Much of her Instagram presence was spent fundraising for an animal rescue she and her friend had founded in Silchar.

> *Urgent! This week, we need four puppy crates and sixty packets of Whiskas for our puppy and cat rescues! Here's the Amazon link. You can send the food directly to us or you can UPI me.*

Messages like this were on her story every couple of weeks. It seemed incredibly transparent because she offered Amazon links and promised an address to send the supplies. Of course it had to be legit. Utsav once bought a large puppy crate off Amazon after a request was made in a story; he even sent it to an Assam address. I have no idea where that puppy crate went or who used it. I imagine many people looked at the Amazon link and felt guilt and laziness: *Why fill out a new shipping address on my Amazon account? I'll just send her the money.*

The first time, I purchased supplies from the Amazon link. After that, I resorted to sending her the money via UPI. After all, she always gave the option of buying through Amazon; it's not like I didn't trust her.

In the years of viewing Sanch's stories, I have seen many minor animal emergencies. I didn't respond to all of them. She often reached her emergency fundraiser goals in a few days, regardless of whether I participated. One time, Sanch posted a story saying that she was a few thousand rupees short for this super sick cat she had picked up. I read it while scrolling in bed after waking up. I got myself out of bed with more purpose and save-the-day energy. I texted her: 'How much are you short, exactly? I'll figure out the rest and ask some friends.'

'5k, that's what the vet said,' she replied.

I sent her 5k. She texted back in a few minutes: 'OMG, you are amazing! ILU.'

Between the texts we shared over Instagram and WhatsApp, Sanch occasionally mentioned the various pets in her life. I remember seeing pictures of what looked like a thin German Shepherd on a terrace as I'd mindlessly swiped through my friends' Instagram stories for the day. She always had a vague story about this dog: sometimes it was her cousin who took care of the dog or it was the dog her father had before he died and now it lived in some relative's house. I am not sure why I never pinned her to specifics because when it comes to animals, especially dogs, I usually want to know everything.

Was my body freezing? It was. It was telling me not to dig. Don't ask for details you are not ready for. Don't ask Sanch specific questions. Protect yourself. Freeze.

I found ways to explain it away. I told myself that not everyone remembers details the way I do. That some stories get fuzzy when grief is involved. That maybe love for animals doesn't always show up in the tidy, obsessive way mine does. I wanted the story to be true more than I wanted it to be confirmed. And so, I let silence fill in the gaps. I mistook my body freezing for fairness. I mistook my doubts for respect. I mistook my body's quiet warning for empathy.

Much of our relationship online on text was a series of rants but when it came to her life, she was equivocal in most of her answers. In the initial year and a half of our online discussions, I never tracked her to be especially prevaricative with her answers. Slightly vague or quick to change the topic? Yes. Slowly but surely. That had tracked. But my body's ability to freeze and render me useless when it came to asking specific questions—my most treasured skill—showed up only when I met her in real life. Sanch as a person right in front of me was familiar but physically muted and unsure compared to her texting persona, which could be described as spilling, ranting, raving, highly intelligent and shit-talking.

A person who rescues dogs and plays with Indies on the street knows when a friendly dog looking for attention and interaction is approaching them.

But then again, a new dog is a new dog. Unfamiliarity breeds caution, no matter how familiar one is with certain animals. Sanch managed to pat Jeera's head and fumble awkwardly to her room.

'Get some good sleep. In the morning, we'll have breakfast and talk, okay? Everything is set up in your room,' I said.

She nodded and oohed and aahed at the sleep mask and snacks I had left on her bed. I had sprayed her pillow covers with lavender. I had done my part.

She shut the guest room door and I breathed a sigh of relief, knowing that I could enjoy going back to sleep without stressing about my new guest. *Great*, I thought. *She's self-sufficient and understands the essential boundaries of being in another person's home at 4 a.m. She's not waiting for me to entertain her.*

~

I must tell you about my obsession with deception.

I have always been obsessed with catfishing stories. I am both moved and annoyed by the length of time people will go without poking obvious holes in the stories told by someone they meet online. This is common when you interact with someone online with the intent to meet, marry and love them but they never show up or meet you. The extraordinary chaos and wicked imagination a catfisher has to deceive a person every day makes me sick. Still, it also gets me super curious about their brains. Do they live in constant fear of being found out? Are they exhausted by their lies? Do they worry when they say something that doesn't add up or do they simply move on to the next lie?

I've watched multiple episodes of MTV's *Catfish: The TV Show*, a somewhat exploitive but entertaining show in which 'social media detectives' help people find out if they have been catfished and then track down their catfisher to expose their real identity. Some catfishers deceive for financial gain; some do it out of loneliness. Some seem to do it because they can exist as someone else in another person's imagination: they feel validated and seen even though the foundation of the relationship is soggy cardboard at best.

And then there are faux-aristocratic, luxury scammers like Shimon Hayut, commonly known as the Tinder Swindler, and Anna Sorokin aka Anna Delvey, who bring out the most jarring emotions in people. Their stories are delectable, a delicious crumb of cake you can't help but pick off the table and put in your mouth. If you were forced to be a scammer, you'd want to be a scammer of this stature.

It's much easier to hate on lonely, mundane, evil catfishers, the ones who bait middle-aged men and women who are widowed, divorced or trapped in the unrelenting boredom of a dead marriage. Their victims have some money but a dwindling sense of self-worth because, well, life is hard. A catfisher offers them something intoxicating, the chance to feel *seen* for the first time. The catfisher allows them to save a lover with affection and money until they inevitably realize it was all a scam.

But sometimes, the truth is even messier. Some victims *know* deep down that the person they're talking to is fake, that their bank account has been drained, that the sweet nothings they're told are well-rehearsed lies. Yet they continue, flipping about like fish pulled out of the water, thrashing for some semblance of safety. They inhale every message like oxygen. And you, rational and detached, might be supremely tempted to ask: *Why? Why are people this stupid? Why can't they see through it? Why are they doing this to themselves?*

The whole truth requires the willingness to look straight into the eyes of our absurdities. You may resonate with fragments of the contradictory nature of humans. Even then, it's hard to comprehend its vast spectrum. Absurdity does not limit itself to individual tolerance.

I know we all live in some form of delusion to survive and, sometimes, it's far safer and practical to maintain this. Deep-throating the senseless reality we live in at all times is not an art any one human can master.

It's hard to cut the bullshit one might endure in a boring, senseless marriage. It's harder still to leave an abusive one. Sometimes, there is no way out of chronic illness and depression; having a fake lover is enough to keep you numb but breathing. Sometimes, it's just a kick, a secret language you get to speak in a world that doesn't allow you to feel important even for a second. Most times, it's a habit, a hit of nicotine or the sweet, vacant lull of Valium—anything that distracts you from the distress of life, even if it's for mere minutes.

What makes me deeply uncomfortable is our affinity to be classist, parochial and plain casteist, even when it comes to scammers. We are so scared of the grossness of being human, our faecal selves, our snotty noses, our messy lives, our deep, deep vulnerabilities, that we do everything to run away from our basest commonalities. Evil is better when it's iconic and glamorized. It's just a fact. We want our misery coated in a layer of glamour. If the ache of being human must be endured, it must have a chance of metamorphosing into urban myth and folklore. If our pain must exist, it ought to be mythologized.

I am no exception to this need. I am both disgusted and delighted by these glamorous scammers. Once they're caught, their stories are memorialized. Even the wounds of their victims bleed gold because the narrative is just that compelling. We find solace and satisfaction in the precise shade of trauma we imagine the victims endured. And the scammers themselves? You know, the Belle Gibson variety, where someone's entire identity is one big medical emergency designed to shake money out of you. I am unsure but bad press may still make them feel validated or worthy of mass consumption. In telling our stories, we ironically give them back some power.

Sanch is a hybrid. Sanch is a part of local folklore. Sanch is a combination of a prosaic lack of empathy and a pronounced set of insecurities. She's much like a catfisher in this way. But she has ambition and youth and they are far too enticing for her to run her game anonymously. She wears her Anna Delvey costume to cover up her mouldy, lonely, tech-bro-core, fake-it-till-you-make-it insecurities. Sanch is a real person. She posted her real face and the actual places she'd been to and the real people she'd met. Except for the parts that she told you. Those were all lies.

~

Sanch was sitting on my guest bed, her long, straight hair spread around her shoulders. At 10 a.m., I had knocked on her door to see if she wanted coffee or breakfast. She was wearing shorts and a crumpled T-shirt, her face bare without a trace of eyeliner or lipstick. This was the most vulnerable I had seen her.

The only physical issue that Sanch had mentioned to me was scoliosis, a condition I could confirm by her appearance. She had a slight hump on her upper back, just below the base of her neck. That morning, the hump was more pronounced as she sat slouched on my bed, rubbing the fabric of the bedsheet as if it were tissue.

She began sharing a part of her life with me, something she often wrote about online. I had hesitated to ask for more details online because I didn't want to come across as overly intrusive but, that day, she wanted to discuss it with me.

Sanch had worked as a sex worker in Calcutta while she was pursuing her undergraduate degree.

'I came out to my dad and told him I was queer and he cut me off for a year. That's when I started doing sex work.

Of course, there was a standard; my clients were all at least middle-class men or rich.'

I nodded ferociously to validate her every word. One small part of my brain registered an abnormal tick: the fact that Sanch had to make sure her sex work had a 'standard' because when she wrote about it online, she wrote in solidarity with all sex workers, even the ones who were far poorer by class or in terms of mainstream good looks. Perhaps it was the way she said it; the context was authentic enough: she wanted me to know that sex workers had a spectrum and that she only did this work with people of a particular class. Fair enough. But it was the way she said it—that was probably what my brain had caught on for a sharp second. Her tone was telling me something else: *listen, I don't fuck poor people; I only worked for upper-class men.* She didn't say that, of course, but it's only now that I can, with profound certainty, tell you that's precisely what she meant.

~

It was probably a few hours after Sanch had told me about her sex work in Calcutta. I had finished my main work-from-home calls for the day while Sanch showered and leisurely got ready. By then, Jeera and Sanch had warmed up to each other; he even sat on her bed, watching her pull her hair into a bun and apply thick eyeliner.

'Jeeru-Jeeru, Jeeru-Jeeru!' She had already found an original, sing-song way to affectionately call him. The wave of discomfort I had felt that morning transformed into bright, rose-tinted ideas about the fun adventures we could have in the next couple of days.

I took her to Church Street, where we walked around, sipping Third Wave coffee from paper cups and pausing randomly for selfies. We talked about our shared views on Bengali culture; we joked about bhodrolok smugness and Bengali upper-caste superiority. Sanch, of course, was the authority on all culture critiques; even though I was so much older than her and had so much more life experience and actual receipts for walking a lot of my talk, I still defaulted to her authority because of her immaculate articulation and her marginalized social location. I now know this was the cruellest thing I allowed Sanch to do to me: making me second-guess my confidence. I had lived multiple lives by the time I met Sanch and was brave enough to confront and live through very challenging circumstances. But with Sanch, I defaulted to idpol (identity politics). I crumpled the vastness of my life into a tiny ball of paper.

A person might be knowledgeable and self-aware but the quality of that perceived intelligence cannot be performed in all contexts.

Intelligence, confidence and self-awareness are not linear. The most successful woman you think you know may not be able to confront physical abuse from an intimate partner. The brilliant gender politics professor you know from your networks may not be able to confront their own family when it comes to their queerness. The most nurturing neighbour auntie you know from childhood can be emotionally negligent to her children. Power, trauma and context continually erode the consistency we think intelligence or personality traits must perform.

These are things I already knew and understood from the various past lives I had lived. But on Church Street, wandering the streets, caffeinated and dressed up, I never paused to think that Sanch would have those inconsistencies in her intelligence or self-awareness. If someone has allowed you to believe they are always performing at the same moral, intellectual and emotional speed, you should know they are wrong. You should worry if you are enraptured by them and nod your head to everything, shrinking yourself entirely.

That night, I made my famous vegan keema curry, a staple in my house. Since giving up meat at the age of twenty-five and then going vegan at thirty-three, I had replaced a favourite beef keema curry my mom used to make when I was a child with soya granules and Shan masala.

Since Sanch used to eat everything before she went vegan a couple of years ago, I thought she would appreciate my spicy meat-replacement curry with white rice and salad. I made a video of her eating it. I had made sure to add potatoes to satisfy the Bengali in her. She said it was delicious but struggled to eat the whole thing because it was too spicy. It could have been the non-meat replacement that disappointed her but, in her defence, Shan masala is spicy AF.

Sanch's stance on animal rights was one of the primary reasons I pedestalled her; she had to be extraordinary because she understood the intersection of animal rights in the context of human oppression in her twenties. She could critique the very bullshit tropes of white or savarna veganism and still make a case for the importance of veganism in intersectional justice work. Regular basics most Indians eat are vegan anyway or can be by simply omitting ghee.

There were very few people in our Instagram groups at that time who were thoroughly anti-caste, anti-capitalism, socialist *and* vegan. Veganism as a social-justice movement entered social media politics with a bang, and it was an obvious threat to many non-vegan anti-oppression writers, primarily because nobody wanted to give up their food habits or have them questioned. It has been the most complex space for me to negotiate as a writer; I've been a non-perfect vegan since 2016 and have fiercely critiqued mainstream vegan tactics while still holding humans accountable to the social-justice movement that veganism must genuinely be about; it is an unmissable part of our collective liberation. Suffice to say, it's a challenging space to be in because it makes both vegans and anti-vegans dislike you.

~

The day before she left Bangalore, I brought Jeera and her to the terrace to enjoy the early November sun.

'You'll actually see Jeera get up and move on the terrace,' I joked.

Sanch stood on the terrace, her straight hair sparkling under the sun. I snatched Jeera's toy rope and started to run around, waiting for him to start chasing me and play tug-of-war. Jeera started with his typical play growl as he grabbed the toy and pulled. Then, I noticed Sanch standing in the corner of the terrace, looking absolutely terrified.

'It's just a play growl ...' I explained.

I stopped pulling; Jeera abruptly let go and squinted in confusion.

'It's dog play; you had a dog, right?' I ask.

'Yeah, I know but my dad used to do all the walking and play stuff.'

The freezing of my body was unmistakable then.

'This is typical dog play behaviour,' I managed to blurt out.

'Yeah, I get it.'

She softened her expression. 'Jeeru-Jeeru,' she squeaked at him as if to make up. He ran towards her, expecting her to chase him. She braced herself in terror until Jeera paused by her, again confused and disappointed.

'Jeera, come here, come and play with this. Sanch is scared; come here,' I called out.

He moved back to me and started to play with his rope again.

Sanch approached us, held the toy and bravely wiggled it in Jeera's face. There, it made sense now. She was able to play with Jeera. I even have a video of it, more so because I wanted to record the truth I wanted Sanch to be: she could play with dogs because she did it all the time. She stopped after a few seconds and walked off to a corner of the terrace. She stood, seemingly dissociating for many seconds, looking vacantly at the horizon. I took that video to prove something, not what was true but what I needed it to be. That she was okay. That I hadn't imagined the connection. That this wasn't strange.

But something in my body flinched. Not loudly. Just enough to know.

She stood apart afterwards, quiet and hollowed out, like she'd left the moment before it even ended.

I saved it as a memory. But it was really a record of unease, my gut trying to speak before I was ready to listen.

CHAPTER 4

It was February 2025. I was in Delhi to spend time with my friend Sana, who had just lost a parent. It hit me that it had been a year since the aftermath of Sanch. It was my first trip to Sana's house in Delhi; she had visited me in Bangalore a couple of times the previous year.

Sana and I are, for the most part, Instagram friends. We met because of shared ideologies and stayed in touch online for eight years before meeting in person. There are a few precious people in my life, like Sana—friends I made online—where there is a risk in believing their curated posts reflect their lived realities. Yet, trust comes easily to me. Especially if someone questions the world, dumbfounded by its absurdities, cruelties and sudden joys.

Sana displayed a pragmatic, compassionate sort of activism in all her posts. During the aftermath of the Sanch scam, she was one of the few online friends who spent hours on the phone with me, helping me regulate my nervous system. When most people were asking, 'How can you trust anyone now unless you've known them for years in real life?', Sana was my proof that trust was still possible. That sometimes, the most soul-expansive care begins with strangers online.

When I arrived at her house on a random Saturday evening, I was delighted and semi-shocked. Everything was photoshoot ready: dust-free, intentional, balanced. Every picture frame had a story, every surface was both beautiful and useful. Even the nightstands had accessories that looked like they were piped on by a pastry artist.

And then, in the middle of this curated calm, Sana threw a question at me that shattered my idea of writing this book.

'Have you talked to Ankur about it? You need to get Ankur's thoughts, no matter how he feels. Even if he hates the idea.'

I swallowed hard. She'd caught me exactly where I needed to be seen.

Ankur and I were on a mutually agreed hiatus. We hadn't spoken in a year. There was too much suffering, and we experienced it in drastically different ways. We were too enmeshed. Too sick with shock.

But love and good faith were never the problems. I just assumed we'd drift back into each other's lives someday—that there'd be some vague future reunion.

But Sana dispelled the fantasy. She's that kind of friend, the one who holds you accountable with love and expects you to follow through.

A friend who points at the cracks in your integrity and waits for you with glue.

At her dining table, I started drafting a message to Ankur. As my fingers moved, I felt that familiar sense of well-being, the muscle memory of our friendship.

And then panic rose in my throat as I pressed send.

Ankur—a man with a vast heart, sharp mind and a quiet, steady humanity, reduced, more often than not, to *Sanch's boyfriend*. The guy who got duped, who, like me, was merely chasing the hope that most humans are good and want to be loved. The man who, against all odds, fell for a garden-variety sociopath.

Ankur was a mirror to my mess and one of my most cherished online friendships, one I almost lost entirely.

I imagine Ankur and me as pieces of stone battered by a sculptor who never intended to shape us. By the end of January 2024, we were misshapen, jagged and left with edges too sharp to be close to each other. Sanch had robbed us in acutely different ways. Sure, she made us weave a net of delusions that came together in collective knots but they eventually broke apart into straggly threads of individual heartbreaks.

I had met Ankur on Instagram as well. The algorithm brought us together, most probably because we're both part of anti-caste animal rights circles. Ankur's Instagram handle juxtaposed his Dalit identity with veganism. He was one of the very first people to stand firm in the domain of animal rights while also talking about the reality of caste and purity politics in India. He made the usual moralistic, often self-righteous savarna vegans upset with his nuanced posts while simultaneously disrupting and annoying anti-caste activists who almost always promoted meat eating as the only way to reclaim identity and smash Brahminical ideas of purity and vegetarianism.

In April 2021, after months of liking each other's posts, Ankur DMed me to tell me he was writing a work of fiction and asked if I was down to help with notes about my journey in writing and publishing.

I don't recall sitting down at a specific time to discuss writing with Ankur but that initial DM started a genuine friendship built on a sense of camaraderie that would have never existed without Instagram.

When we first met, Ankur was almost thirty years old and living in Hyderabad for work. Over our initial chats, I learned that Ankur was born and raised in a village in Maharashtra. He attended a Marathi-medium school and didn't learn English until he was in college.

When I first learned this, I laid it on too thick with the praise. I may have even veered into condescending territory without meaning to. But the truth was his writing was sharp, funny and surprisingly tender. Still, Ankur never made a big deal of it; he owed it to his relentless reading, book after book, in college, until he cracked the code. He built a voice that carried the ease, wit and range of someone born into urban English privilege, even though that world wasn't handed to him on a platter.

Very early on in our online friendship, I asked if he'd be interested in doing an Instagram live on the differences between caste-based vegetarianism and veganism. He replied with cautious enthusiasm. Ankur always spoke to me with a gentle reticence, as if holding back a larger desire to break through. I was the overenthusiastic, encouraging writer friend, always ready to take on the world with big ideas. On the other hand, he was the shy but earnest buddy, quietly validating my need to inspire while letting me take centre stage in conversations. Our chats online formed a comfortable pattern; I'd climb onto my emotional soapbox, ranting about the world and how we could all be trailblazers if only we stopped nodding along to a world that would always make us uncomfortable. Ankur would respond with textual nods and soft affirmations.

Ankur loved cricket so much that he once told me he tried to get into a college based on how much cricket he could play. He bunked a good portion of his classes to go out and play.

'I studied chemical engineering for two years, dropped out, played cricket at an academy, lost interest in the competitive and extreme discipline it required, injured my shoulder and then went to Mumbai to get a BA.'

He was always playing catch-up in college. Trying to feel culturally relevant by watching old sitcoms like *F.R.I.E.N.D.S.* that had already gone through five cycles of internet cancellation and revival before he ever had access to the show. He'd collect e-books on his Nokia and temporarily escape reality through fantasy and science fiction. The culture in college was vastly different from that of the Marathi-medium school he had attended.

'People looked different, talked differently and smelled good. I became increasingly aware of how I presented myself,' he told me during one of our WhatsApp chats.

Somehow, Ankur never submitted to the ragging culture that was omnipresent and spread thickly throughout his college experiences. He resisted bullying without being heroic or theatrical about it. 'I never bought into it; I mean, I am generally a scaredy-cat but I am a brave scaredy-cat.'

This oxymoron captures how I've always seen Ankur. His educational struggles, intense passions and obsessive fixations are almost always paired with a sudden nosedive that goes against sustaining any long-term dream. It reveals his attention deficit hyperactivity disorder (ADHD), depression and anxiety that seem to shadow him wherever he goes.

But I see other parts he neglects in his own narrative. Ankur rarely sees the whole arc of what he's survived: the sheer act of enduring, of pushing forward despite overwhelming odds. That, I think, is the quiet bravery he refers to. A fleeting flicker of resistance and resilience that he's only partially aware of, even as it burns at his core.

By the time I met Ankur, I'd only seen the glimmers of his past passion by tracking his rabid enthusiasm for cricket on Instagram, where he would take a brief break from his usual political stories to report about some team winning. My brain would categorize these stories under the larger subcategory of his other interests; if you asked me today which cricket team Ankur is most likely to support and potentially get emotional about, I couldn't tell you.

But I will tell you that I don't think online friendships are any less dangerous than real ones. Friendships are primarily constructed on proximity: school neighbourhoods, college and work. But social media gave us seatbelt extenders; sure, friendship is still based on proximity to class and common language but the internet opened more potential to create bonds over particular passions, interests or causes or even fanning over a niche micro-celebrity. I don't see online friendships as any more dangerous than the strangers or community members we let into our real lives. Most abuse, quiet scandals and traumatic events are caused by the seemingly innocuous orthodoxy of the everyday.[1] It's not the stranger in the alley, it's a familiar touch in a familiar room. One in three married women in India experience intimate partner violence in their lifetime[2] and, culturally, a grand majority of women who suffer don't even tell anyone about it. It's woven into the daily rhythms of life: the kitchen arguments, the sibling jokes that bruise, the silent debts we carry in families. Even most financial scams happen quietly within the family in the form of taking advantage of elderly parents or using the power of trust to manipulate funds.[3]

Most of us have wronged people by being spineless bystanders to the norm. Most of us have endured pain and confusion from the people we're supposed to know.

Curiously, the Instagram live talk on veganism would be the first time Ankur and I would talk in person. Up till then, we had only texted.

I took my camera time seriously and got ready several hours in advance.

I had washed my tediously thick and curly hair, scrunched it with curl cream and put half of it in a casual bun, scattering the other half on my back and shoulders. I smeared on some lip gloss, ran kajal under my eyes, hopped online and asked

Ankur to join. He looked just like his pictures—thick hair, wearing a casual tee and that reserved, quietly handsome smile. But his body language, with a slight slouch in his shoulders and pauses between our greetings, was shyer and more hesitant than the bold, self-assured energy of his online posts. Still, the dynamic between us, his presence and mine, felt like a continuation of the larger pattern we had already established on WhatsApp. His points came across with quiet conviction: direct, confident in theory but paced and deliberate. I was high-strung, often stumbling over my words, tumbling through thoughts faster than I could catch them.

Our conversation was earnest; we had no big followings to speak of nor were we interested in making a mainstream impact; we were simply trying to voice out the major conflicts in the Indian vegan movement. It felt exactly as intended: two new friends with a common interest who were unafraid to share their thoughts and opinions online. Our little online project acted as the auspicious ceremony that solidified the foundation of our friendship.

But other people were watching. We all watch each other on social media; we have subgroups, frenemies and people we admire secretly and not-so-secretly. No matter what you say on the internet, some people make assumptions and get triggered. Some people resonate with you secretly or in the comments, if you're lucky. Others feel threatened, ashamed or repelled. You can't control what people think about you and social media has proven this adage in extraordinarily incontestable ways.

But what if some people aren't merely observing you; what if they're calculating from the corners? What if they don't just absorb your world view but rehearse and mimic it until you mistake reflection for resonance? What if they're metabolizing your kindness, your trust, your softness and very human, sacred contradictions? What happens when your already paper-thin online vulnerabilities start absorbing *them*, their projections, their rehearsed empathy almost imperceptibly, until your edges blur? It feels like your integrity, what you once believed was unshakeable, becomes soggy, warped and eventually unrecognizable.

What if you were never seen at all but studied?

~

If you're someone who instinctively recoils at the word 'vegan', you're probably reacting less to the lifestyle itself and more to the moral righteousness and total lack of nuance that often comes with the loudest voices online, especially from new converts swinging in with all the blunt force of a freshly lit cause.

Between 2014 and 2016, a wave of vegan influencers from around the world began gaining serious traction, especially on Instagram.[4] Hashtags like #vegan, #plantbased and #veganfoodporn surged as veganism became less about political resistance and more about aesthetic curation: smoothie bowls, minimalist kitchens and influencer-driven lifestyle templates. As their followers grew, more minor cults of belief started to form, each with its own rules, rituals and slightly different take on what 'true' veganism meant.

The exact practices and forms of advocacy varied wildly depending on who you were listening to. There were the raw vegans, the alkaline vegans, the fruitarians and the militant health evangelists who argued veganism was the ultimate weight-loss and detox solution. And like most things that pass through the algorithm, this version of veganism travelled globally—landing in urban India around 2016 to 2018.[5]

As with many trends that shape the market here, the people driving this new social-justice movement were mostly the elite: the so-called upper caste, city-bred, English-speaking Indians who had finally discovered the horrors of the dairy industry and industrialized animal cruelty, information that Dalit, Bahujan and Adivasi communities had lived alongside and laboured under for generations.[6] The veganism that gained social capital in India was rarely connected to caste-based labour, food insecurity or regional histories but it often mimicked the Western-influencer aesthetic, polished and conveniently disconnected from the politics of who grows, cleans and prepares our food.[7]

By the time mainstream veganism hit urban Indian society, I had already been a vegetarian for seven years.

I grew up eating beef, pork, chicken and seafood, likely due to being raised by a Mangalorean Catholic mother and a Bengali Hindu father in America for the first ten years of my life. By the time I was twenty-five, I had given up eating meat because I emotionally felt for all the animals that were on my plate. Veganism was more challenging and I had never really considered the broader social justice ideas that veganism, at its core, challenges us all with.

This might sound like a detour but the politics of food and my journey with it are inextricably intertwined with the absurd amount of trust I unconsciously gave to Sanch.

After being a vegetarian for seven years, I turned vegan in 2016, years before I met Ankur or Sanch. And like anyone newly swept into a cause, I had plenty of opinions. But mostly, I felt lonely. Lonely in the face of the loud, binary rhetoric many vegan activists clung to, rhetoric stripped of caste and class analysis, devoid of any context around disability or mental health. I wrote an extended essay on Medium titled 'I Am Vegan but Veganism Is Arbitrary and Inconsistent'.[8] That essay had me trolled for weeks. Vegans called me a meat apologist, a fake vegan, etc. As for the non-vegans, they didn't care either way.

I was bored and annoyed with the rhetoric online, except for a few vegan friends like Sana, who would resonate and agree with the lack of nuance in the current animal rights space. And then came Ankur, years later, with a bang. His posts were oddly confident for a person taking such unpopular stances. He was saying: I am Dalit, I am vegan and there are meaningful conversations we need to have around these areas.

At first, Sanch had developed her online presence with anti-caste talk, being pro-sex workers' rights and shedding light on the reality of transpeople's lives. But slowly, I saw her post about animal rights too, brazenly, sometimes in fun, zany, unhinged ways that probably stopped all trolls from saying anything back. Sanch's typical shots at non-vegans would look like this:

> Ya'll whine about veganism being too expensive? Fuck you, eat your dal, rice, veggies and call it a day! Tum log Zomato, Swiggy se roj order karte ho, aur phir bolte hain ki veganism is too expensive [You people order daily from Zomato and Swiggy and then say veganism is too expensive].

I'd reply with fire or laughter emoticons, goading her on and enjoying the way she blatantly attacked all the social-justice activists who claimed to be intersectional but avoided animal rights at all costs.

By 2022, a few friends from our circle had quietly branched off, forming one-on-one friendships and small subgroups. When Sanch and I first started chatting online, our connection revolved around me hyping up her hot takes on animal rights, trans rights, queer politics and the complex caste and regional politics of Assam. Around the same time, she and Ankur became fast online besties. I'd see them tag each other in their stories and their comments on each other's posts.

Honestly, who wouldn't back up Sanch? She was magnetic, opinionated, clever and grounded in all the right causes.

Ankur later told me he didn't really have a crush on her back then. Still, he thought she was cool. She was a fellow marginalized person speaking out about animal rights. Through her posts and DMs, Sanch introduced Ankur to queer theory and communism. Knowing Ankur, he would've been in awe of her and even a little intimidated, probably in equal measure.

A good portion of my admiration and faith in Sanch came from her ability to write posts that allowed for ambiguity and social context while still illustrating the moral clarity of being pro-animal rights. Or perhaps I had projected my need for validation on to her: I was right all along; animal rights are necessary but yes, the current vegan movement reeks of exclusivity. Sanch allowed me to project. But Ankur let me resonate. I couldn't tell them apart at the time.

When does the ability to discuss intersectional issues with nuance (delivered in a slightly awkward, matter-of-fact way) get flattened by online culture into armchair diagnoses about neurodivergence? And when does that very same cultural intelligence begin to resemble something sharper, more performative, something that edges into the territory of sociopathic detachment?

I have some answers today but most can't be put into words.

I know Ankur had the gift of nuance but he didn't easily have the other qualities that Sanch demonstrated. As I've told you, Ankur was reticent, quiet and fumbled to place his emotions when we chatted online or on the phone. He was reasonable when questioned, accepted his limitations and almost always deferred to me when we weighed the emotional dramas of the internet or talked about life and its unlimited challenges.

There were material realities to these differences, too. My social and education capital far outweighed his. His caste location and small-town beginnings were experiences I had never embodied. It shouldn't have been surprising that the person who had clawed his way through India's discriminatory education system and managed to filter out all the 'small-town' giveaways in his writing would still be hesitant in the face of women like me.

I was bad at school but could code-switch between American and neutral Bangalorean English accents. By the time I was thirty, I was fortunate enough to have travelled to over fifteen countries and more than thirty states in the USA and worked a range of atypical jobs that gave me fluency in diverse cultures and subcultures.

This came at a cost. By the time I was thirty-three, I had lived through chronic depression, two divorces and the suicide of a loved one. Physically, I had moved from New York to Orlando by the time I was ten years old. I'd spent my formative years, from the age of ten to eighteen, in Bangalore. Then, I lived different lives as a young adult in Colorado and San Francisco, only to come back to Bangalore in my late twenties. It is stunningly clear to me today that the instability and vastness of my experiences allow me to connect with people who feel a deep need to be a part of something. A desire to fit in while subsequently wanting to burn the very paradigm that makes you want to fit in.

I recognized the wayward nonconformist in Ankur. Except he didn't have the same luxuries I did. Risking his life on a career in writing or pure advocacy could jeopardize his basic existence and sever all financial and social opportunities that his family had envisioned for him. The louder voice in his head would tell him to just get a government job and everything would be okay. Keep your head down and study for the small number of government jobs in this country. Things like writing, entrepreneurship and creative liberty, those were for folks who could play with risk.

So, why was Sanch able to seemingly break every rule, even as a marginalized queer orphan? Didn't she have even more to lose, especially as a woman?

Over the months that ranged from the end of 2022 to 2023, our friendship grew and the three of us created a WhatsApp group. Our discussions became more playful and dramatic when discussing the people who disliked us on the internet. We made jokes about our collective trauma. Had Sanch made notes of my bias toward dark humour? We both made dead dad jokes all the time because, well, both our dads were dead.

Sanch would reveal layers of herself and expect them to land like well-known movie lines. She prompted us.

'My dad asked me to forgive him from his deathbed; he held my hands and cried for forgiveness.'

And we'd ask for more details.

'I can't afford that right now but I will once my dad's health insurance kicks in next month.'

And we'd ask for more details.

'I got into King's College in London last year with a partial scholarship but couldn't go.'

And we'd ask for more details.

However, the details were scattered, disjointed and tangential. My usual appetite for relentless and intrusive questioning was far more subdued when it came to Sanch. There was an internal dialogue I had with myself, which blocked me from being obnoxiously unrelenting when it came to more details.

Sanch had a kind of blunt openness when it came to sex, bodies, trauma and family toxicity. At the time, it felt disarmingly transformative. But now, I see it more as a device. A shock-and-awe missile she launched into conversations before anyone could ask real questions. It short-circuited your instincts. You were meant to be impressed, maybe even silenced. And if you dared to probe deeper, you self-censored because you'd immediately feel like you were exploiting her courage to say anything at all.

Sanch took up space with her narrative which came out of her in sudden bursts, not in one cohesive timeline, which, for the most part, is natural. The older you get, the less inclination you have to chronologically contextualize your conversations.

Imagine if your life were like hers? She grew up with an abusive, mentally ill mother who died in a car accident when Sanch was sixteen and then a father who died from cancer during the pandemic when she was just twenty-six. We could only hope to survive and thrive the way Sanch seemed to. But that wasn't the most fascinating thing about her; after all, tragedy is relative and there are people who have endured more.

Perhaps my fascination with Sanch was the fact that her ever-growing collection of marginalized labels never stopped her from wanting to help others. She chatted with people online, acting primarily as the wise shoulder to cry on. She'd offer solace and solidarity to queer people who were kicked out of their biological family homes. She'd engage in her DMs with guys who were trying to be 'better men'. She even took the time to run a fundraiser for a woman who had come to her house looking for work. Sanch had detailed that the woman had an income of only Rs 800 a month and was mistreated at the home she worked in. Apart from helping animals, Sanch even became an essential part of fundraising for Silchar during the Assam floods in 2022. I mean, there were pictures. There were stories. Sanch was the exception. She could do it all.

One day in 2023, rather suddenly, she told Ankur and me she wanted to move to Hyderabad. She was disenchanted by the political science degree she had received at Jadavpur University in Calcutta a couple of years ago. She wanted to start as an undergraduate again and pursue psychology, and she had found the perfect college in Hyderabad.

If Ankur and I registered the oddity of this, we didn't speak of it. First of all, if you have an undergraduate degree in political science—which, according to her, she passed with flying colours—you don't need to redo your undergraduate degree; you can just apply for a master's programme in psychology. But Sanch was always up for doing things from 'scratch', as she called it.

Ankur had just rented an apartment in Hyderabad with a friend. However, his roommate was planning to move out and he'd soon have an extra room. Around the same time, in late 2022, Sanch moved to Hyderabad. She found a paying guest (PG) accommodation run by a Bengali woman, 'who is, of course, upper caste,' she said, supplemented with the eyeroll emoticon she reserved for telling you she was two steps ahead of the oppressor.

Trouble followed, predictably.

Within weeks, Sanch had declared herself vindicated, the righteous survivor of casteist, classist tyranny. Her victory came fast and loud; as always, she was the underdog heroine who had outsmarted yet another petty villain.

It was around then that her Instagram stories took a new turn. She began hinting at a crush, someone in Hyderabad, someone she couldn't confess to.

'What if he doesn't like me that way?' she wrote in one story, in lowercase letters, feigning softness.

My eyebrow lifted involuntarily. Until that point, her narrative had been emphatically queer—loud declarations of preferring 'pussy over dick any day', stories of dating women and calls to abolish binaries entirely. There were brief, slippery mentions of being trans. But she often followed them with the assertion that a trans man didn't need to change anything about a visibly female-presenting body. It was a radical idea in theory and one I wanted to believe in. When I once asked what her pronouns were, she replied with a grin: 'You can call me anything you want. You get me.' At the time, I was stupid enough to take that as a compliment.

And I did think I got her, until moments like these, when the ground quietly shifted under my feet, when the story changed again. When what was once radical became suddenly … convenient.

I typed furiously to her story: 'Who do you have a crush on?'

She responded with her classic: 'Heheheheh.'

I goaded her.

'It's Ankur,' she finally admitted.

My heart swelled with love and excitement. My two favourite online people had a chance to be together. They would be perfect together. Sanch and Ankur were gaining small but consistent traction online, writing about being Dalit and vegan. They would be the ideal advocacy couple.

But even then, I was happier for Ankur. He was palpably lonely, always trying to fit in and find companionship. He loved the idea of love and what it could mean for him. His relationships had never really extended beyond online chatting and he was too shy to express his desire for love but I had felt it numerous times.

It only took a few days. I got reports from both Ankur and Sanch. She admitted to him over text that she had a crush on him and Ankur, who had up until now thought of them as just friends, felt, *Wow, could I be that special to someone like Sanch?*

She went to his apartment, talked about it, sealed it with a kiss and then, before I could ask her for an update, Sanch announced it to the world on Instagram.

> Ankur and I are together.
>
> Sanch's Happy Era

I put up a story, almost to show off that I was close to their love story and how happy I was. I look back now and see how cringeworthy my celebration was, like a stereotypical

Indian mother happy that her kid has finally relented and found a partner.

But stories have a way of slipping out of your hands, especially the ones you most want to believe.

Over the next few months, Sanch's stories about her Brahmin Bengali landlady got weirder. Sanch had told her landlady she had a Dalit boyfriend (why?) and the landlady was uncomfortable. Sanch seemed to enjoy her toxic reactions.

'But doesn't she know you are Dalit and tribal too?' I asked.

'No! Because I can speak that bhodro Bengali well; she has no clue.'

Red flag. Why would she be proud that she could masquerade as a Brahmin but out her boyfriend just for kicks?

Welcome to the contradictory clownshow of our friendship. It's a tragicomedy scripted by Sanch, accepted by Ankur and me with the kind of blind faith reserved for manipulated fools. We didn't read the fine print. Maybe we never wanted to. By the time we realized we were characters, not co-authors, it was too late.

Asking questions doesn't help; it'll only reveal that you still think there's a version of this story where someone gets out unhurt. So, I stayed silent.

Back in Sana's apartment, I thought about the message I had sent Ankur. This time, I was the hesitant, shy person. In my message, I had gently asked if he would want to be a part of this book. I had also asked if we could renew our friendship.

His consent would make or break the way I could tell my story. It could also renew or further obliterate my relationship with him. But Sana was right, I had to reach out to him. My panic was mixed with awkwardness. We hadn't talked in a year and now I felt like the exploiter, messaging him just to give him a heads-up about my writing plans.

Ankur's text came back within a few minutes of me pressing send. I went outside to the balcony and sucked on my vape in preparation.

> Hi Rheea. No, I haven't been doing well. And no, I don't want you to write about this. I don't want you ever to mention me and I most certainly don't want to be in the public eye. As for reconnecting, I wish we could but I think we both are handling this very differently, so no. No to everything.

CHAPTER 5

1990, Daytona Beach, Florida

I stood in front of the ocean, my little feet digging snugly into the sugar sand. The photos show that my hair was short but thick. I was the brown-skinned child with her brown parents just inches away, anxious that I had wandered too close to the water. The white folk were more carefree. Their kids ran wild, kicking up clumps of wet sand. Their mothers wore bikinis while my mother wore shorts.

What I remembered most were the elegantly bloated mermaid-blue creatures that lay across the shore like fallen Disney characters. Everyone at Daytona Beach knew about the Portuguese man o' war. They were deadly beauties. A sting wouldn't kill you but it would make you writhe in pain. Avoiding a man o' war was a matter of luck, fate and probability. If you wanted to get your feet wet, jump the ocean's pulse while your parents clutched your hands and gently lifted you into the splash of each wave, you had to risk it; those ballooned creatures could collide with your legs, your chest, even your face if you went deep enough.

Daytona Beach was peppered with patrol vehicles, like airport carts but with thick sand-gliding tyres. Lifeguards drove around, topless and sun-seared, orange-chested and white-skinned.

It was likely a false memory, retroactively embroidered with what I came to know, but I always felt I would be stung. And I was. I barely remember the pain itself. I cried. My face crumpled. My father pulled me out of the water and sat me down on the shore. I remembered the beach patrol rolling up, a white guy mumbling, 'Ah, gotcha today!' before pouring vinegar on my leg. I've held this moment like a trophy ever since. The delicate, dangerous monsters I adored had validated my adoration with their sting.

All my life, I thought they were jellyfish. But as I sat in Bangalore in 2025, recalling those shimmering Florida days from more than three decades ago, I finally looked them up. It turned out the Portuguese man o' war weren't jellyfish at all. They only pretended to be.

They were siphonophores, a strange and eerie class of organism. What appeared to be a single being was actually a colony of genetically identical individuals, each with its role, fused into the illusion of unity. They could not survive alone. And even together, they weren't quite whole. They drifted, directionless, moved not by will but by wind and current.

Had I always been in awe of these creatures or did they become unforgettable only after they hurt me?

WhatsApp voice message from Sanch, 2023

You know what, after thinking deeply, I know it's fucking 2 a.m. … but listen. Every other friend who has backstabbed me, like, you know some of the people I'm talking about … I've always given them something. Emotional support, talking them down from killing themselves. I can't even tell you what I've done, not because I expected anything in return but because I wanted them to know I loved them and wanted the best for them. And that was just totally disregarded.

So, I think it was hard for me to get close to you, even though you were trying to build a connection. I couldn't because you didn't ask anything from me. Instead, you were helping me, doing things for me. And it was so hard for me to accept. I was even suspicious of you.

Like, there's this new person I met and she wants to meet me. And I'm already at the point where I'm thinking: why does she want to meet me? What's her angle? I've become so mistrustful because of the past. But I've realized now … it's scary for me to accept that maybe someone could love me for who I am … That maybe a friend could want to stand up for me, expect nothing in return, just because they know I'd do the same for them. It's a wild feeling, yeah, Rheea. Thank you. I don't even know what to say. I'm just ... making observations. Right, Ankur?

Ankur's voice cut in: 'Yes, we are very, very grateful you're in our lives.'

Sanch's voice returned: 'Yeah! Meow-meow. Bye!'

I played the message in bed the next morning. I wasn't entirely surprised to see a voice note from Sanch; she'd sent them in the middle of the night before. But I noticed the length. It was longer than usual. Her voice began calm, deliberate. Then it softened, took on that babyish lilt she often slipped into, before dipping into a more grounded baritone halfway through. By the end, her vulnerability got the better of her and she retreated again into the baby voice, almost as if to shield herself.

It felt like a homecoming. Sanch was the friend I believed I could fix with my overbearing positivity and relentless faith in her. I thought I could crack the shell she'd built to survive the world's graphic cruelties. Of course she couldn't trust as easily as I did. I believed that if I kept showing up, cheering her on with admiration and awe, offering her the kind of respect she wasn't used to, even though I'd lived more, seen more, it would eventually earn me her complete trust. Her faith. Her love.

So much had already happened in my life; how was it possible that someone just twenty-six years old, someone I hadn't even met in person yet, could occupy such a vast space in the architecture of my emotional world? Here I was, watching a universe of legitimacy form around her presence. In that moment, my online life folded in on itself, forming something whole. Ankur and Sanch were together. Love had stitched them back into themselves and perhaps that same love had softened something in Sanch, enough for her to see what I had always tried to show her—that my love for her was steady, complete and just as foundational as any of the answers we spent our lives chasing. Belonging. That's what it was about.

For me, this was just the beginning. Of what, I couldn't say exactly. But something had cracked open, a deep search for proof that good faith, radical intelligence and tenderness were not just virtues but the very point. The purpose. That all the irregular, fantastically diverse experiences of being alive somehow funnelled towards the same home: connection.

A circle had completed itself in my mind. One part of my life, though lived entirely online, had reached some kind of fruition.

I held back in my response to Sanch. I didn't want to flood her with saccharine thanks. We had always kept things cool or at least emotionally agile. This time, she had chosen to be vulnerable. I knew I had to meet it with resonance, not overkill. I've always been hyper-attuned to people and their thresholds for intimacy. Too much mirroring, too much emotion and people tend to recoil. I know how to bend myself into a comforting shape for others. That shape often costs me. It drains me to the point where I need long periods of retreat, where I collapse into my own silence. I suspect it's worn down my nervous system in ways I can't fully map yet.

But still, I wouldn't undo it. I wouldn't trade in this obsessive earnestness, this desire to offer safety, this compulsion to trust even when I shouldn't. Because that same tenderness, that same naivety, is also what builds me. It is the muscle that creates the possibilities of my existence. I wouldn't want to be anyone else. That much, I know for sure.

Delhi/Bangalore

2025

I read and reread Ankur's message as I stood in Sana's balcony. His response crushed me. I wasn't surprised though. I knew he'd be reluctant, intensely so, at best. He had far more to lose. His credibility, both online and offline, came with repercussions, with layers of embarrassment that couldn't survive public scrutiny like mine could. I had already been chronicling my life online and offline for years with very little restraint.

Maybe the only sign of a living friendship is its ability to survive the most absurdly difficult times with good faith, with the belief that the other person never intended harm, shame or forced a retelling of trauma. Maybe a real friendship is one that remembers what brought two people together in the first place: the implicit trust that we could resonate with each other while holding space for our extraordinary differences in temperament, in life paths and in how fast or slow we metabolized our pain.

Ankur's past year had been a complete shitstorm. Sanch's betrayal, her calculated, mind-bending lies had shattered something sacred. They confirmed the bitter truths the world had trained him to believe. What was the point of opening up when it's to people who turn your worst pain into a spectacle?

After all, you're reading this because it's compelling. Human curiosity feeds off our shadows; we're drawn to the chaos, the brokenness, the audacity of deception. We don't want to admit it but trauma makes us feel vindicated. It explains something primal in all of us.

As a writer, I own this hunger. My fascination with the darker folds of humanity is not passive, it's mirrored by a willingness to turn the gaze inward. I've made a life of saying things that make me uncomfortable, of exposing tender, embarrassing truths. I used to be the person too scared to ask for a glass of water, afraid of being a burden. I used to imagine I could never write or speak publicly about my personal life. Yet, I've spent most of my thirties doing precisely that online, for strangers, for myself. It was my salvation, a reclamation of a childhood spent gagged by inadequacy, confusion and the surreal hypocrisy of adults.

In most friendships, I am the inconvenient mirror. The one who makes it harder to keep up the performance. I name things in real time. I point out the absurd, weird, deeply human things we partake in every day. People run from that. And I've run too. I've hurt people. I unravel when I have silenced myself for too long; when I tolerate the polite, the performative, my body rebels. My soul has been violated. I rarely accept a war with myself.

But Ankur stays.

Yes, at first, he was furious I wanted to write any of this. He resisted, viscerally. But he didn't vanish. He let my presence grate on him. He sweated through it. His anxiety flattened him but he rose, again and again. Because Ankur has strength and beneath his hesitation was a powerful honesty waiting to detonate.

Over the early months of 2025, we found ourselves in our shared truth: that we were both willing to trust each other, even when trust felt like a foreign language.

Looking back now, I know this: Sanch's voice note wasn't the full circle moment of trust and patience I'd been looking for. Ankur was.

And he still is.

Because the story isn't over. The discomfort is still here.

But so are we.

~

It was March 2025 when Ankur and I finally decided to revisit the past. We went over it in long, winding WhatsApp chats, exchanging fragments, challenging each other's memories, stitching the pieces together from opposite ends of the same wreckage.

One evening, Ankur's voice note dropped into my phone with a familiar crackle.

'Start from the beginning,' I asked him. 'When do you really remember noticing her online?'

There was a pause before his reply came through. His voice was steady but I could hear the heaviness in it.

'I'd just joined Instagram and was a couple of months into it when I started following her profile. I knew her for about two years online. She told me she could relate to my pain—she had her own. Bullied in school, shamed for developing early, punished by teachers. She faced caste discrimination all her life for being tribal. Her home life was worse. Her mother had schizophrenia and treated her horribly. Her father was distant, uninvolved. Never ensured she had money to survive college. She said she turned to sex work to get by. When he was dying of blood and bone cancer, she told me he apologized to her but she didn't accept it.'

Ankur's words tumbled out like they'd been waiting to be said out loud.

'I admired her tenacity. What she'd survived and still managed to achieve. I didn't have a fundamental understanding of the political complexities of the world back then. In college, when my upper-caste classmates said it was unfair that I got in through reservation, I didn't know how to respond. I didn't have the words, the knowledge or the confidence. When a teacher once said, "You're smart, I'd never have guessed you're from an SC [scheduled caste] background," I just nodded. I didn't want to be cast out of the group.'

He sighed, soft but sharp. 'It was only after joining Instagram that I started reading political literature. It felt liberating, to finally understand the deeper layers, to have the vocabulary to express what I'd always felt. And Sanch was that for a lot of us online, right? She was already doing the work—protesting, getting arrested, getting beaten. She was the one we looked up to.'

'She really was,' I texted back. 'That's exactly how I felt about her too.'

'But then things changed fast. We met.'

Ankur told me he met her in August 2022. She hadn't told him she was coming to Hyderabad until the last moment.

'We were already "best friends" by then,' he said, with a hint of disbelief. 'She declared it one day, mid-conversation: "We're best friends now." I remember thinking—*we are?* There's no blueprint for that, right? But I was just happy someone like her considered me her best friend.'

There had been other labels before that—'online friends', 'someone I trust when I'm drunk' and then the gold star: 'All men are trash but not you'. Ankur had been one of the two men she'd granted that exception.

'She gave me that badge,' he said. 'It felt like an honour. My online circle back then was the radical kind—strong identity politics, unforgiving. Anyone who made a mistake should be burned at the stake. I hated myself for being a man. I was ashamed of it. So, getting the "not trash" tag from two self-proclaimed feminists? That was a big deal for me.'

I told him she'd done something similar with me, just in a different flavour—positioning me as the 'savarna she could trust', someone who wasn't like the rest.

'And another thing,' Ankur said. 'You know what I loved about her and I know you did too—she was vocal about animal rights. It was rare back then. Most leftists ignored it but not her. She said she'd learned about animal rights from the other guy on the "not trash" list.'

There was a pause in the chat. He added, 'In retrospect, I don't think she actually read the literature she flaunted. She knew enough to pretend, enough to pass. This all started during the lockdown, right? Meeting people online was the only option.'

I hadn't thought of that before. I remembered one of her visits, watching her 'fast read' through a copy of Ashoka Mody's *India Is Broken* at my house. She'd summarized chunks of it within an hour—said she'd finished more than half the book in a couple of hours. At the time, I'd been impressed by her speed. Looking back, I could see the pattern—her need to consume literature superficially but with enough contextual skill to pass as deeply read.

'Honestly, no matter which way we look at it, she was brilliant,' I said.

'She was,' Ankur agreed. 'She couldn't stand not knowing things—even right from the beginning. Whether it was a difficult video game, the ending of a movie, a book, she had to know. I only really noticed this when we lived together... but I'm skipping ahead.'

He told me how, quite suddenly, she'd announced she was moving to Hyderabad to study psychology. Political science wasn't giving her the opportunities she wanted. She wanted to start over.

'I still remember the first time I met her,' he said, his voice softening. 'Those memories still make me smile, until they're rudely interrupted by what came after.'

A few weeks later, she had started telling people she had a crush on someone. And then one day, she had told him: it was him.

'I'd always liked her from afar but didn't want to risk the friendship. So, when she confessed, it was a pleasant surprise. I told her we could give it a shot.'

'I remember that!' I said. 'I was so, so happy for you.'

'The initial months were beautiful,' Ankur continued. 'She was everything I wanted and more. She declared her love publicly, told everyone we were dating. My days were suddenly full of joy. I had hope again. She made me believe in a future. She made me feel like we could carve out a world of our own, away from all the cruelty and trauma. She said all she wanted was for me to be happy.

'She made me feel seen. I didn't need to chase love any more. She reminded me of the good I'd done, of who I really was. She told me I needed to stop hating myself to heal. And with her, my shame began to fade. For the first time in a long time, I felt free.

'She knew exactly what to say. Nothing of what she said was new, you follow enough "woke" people online, you learn the words. But what matters is who says them and when. She was the person I loved the most. Her love was what I needed the most. And she knew it. She knew me too well. My past, my desires, my pain.'

They talked about marriage. Ankur told his parents she was the one. His mostly orthodox family welcomed her into their home, a rare move before marriage. They went on a family trip together.

Then came the pressure to get married quickly. Ankur resisted. She didn't. She saw her opening and told his mother she wanted the same. He caved. Engagement now, marriage later. But dates had already been set.

'She immediately posted about it on social media,' Ankur said. 'I didn't like it. But everyone seemed so happy. I pushed the feeling down.'

The calls, the congratulations, the flood of approval from all directions.

'I pushed the feeling down further. Maybe, I thought, this was for the best ...'

But not even the 'perfect' honeymoon period was as lovely as Ankur had first told me. Later on, he told me about the smaller things, like the Goa trip early in their relationship. The first crack in the mask came from something so small, it still felt absurd to repeat out loud.

They were at a beach café with Ankur's roommate, sun burning the wood of the tables, air heavy with salt. Sanch handed him her glasses while she posed for photos with the roommate. He took them without thinking, fingers closing around the lens instead of the frame. A careless gesture. A smudge waiting to happen.

What followed was instant. An insult, maybe two. He didn't remember the exact words, only the sting of them, sharp, humiliating. The roommate joined in immediately, seizing the chance to pile on. *Disrespectful.* That was the word Sanch used, and the roommate echoed it. Not careless, not clumsy. *Disrespectful.*

Ankur told me his body went rigid. His instincts screamed at him to run but instead he sat there, stunned. He hadn't expected such hostility over something so small. He wanted to say sorry for the smudge but the way the situation had unfolded soured the already salted air. It was as if he'd done something unforgivable, as if a fingerprint on glass was violence.

He refused to apologize at first. For hours, Sanch carried a sour expression on her face, like a shadow she wanted him to see. The roommate, meanwhile, looked at him with the kind of disdain that said he didn't deserve Sanch at all. And Ankur knew Sanch noticed; she knew she used her power, knew she let the roommate side with her to corner him.

The suffocation grew unbearable. His mind folded in on itself, replaying the moment, wondering if he had in fact done something wrong. Eventually, he apologized, not because he believed it but because he couldn't breathe under their combined disapproval. He wanted it to end. And then, she smiled faintly, almost pleased, and said, 'This was our first fight.'

Ankur told me he felt it in his bones: the way she said it was wrong. Like she had won something. Like the entire scene had been orchestrated for this moment. He realized, even then, that the fight wasn't real. It had been manufactured. Disingenuous. A performance designed to make him bend.

It made me think about my own quieter journey with Sanch, the stuff that was not declared on Instagram stories or in happy group chats.

Everything I knew about Sanch came in fragments: text messages, voice notes, late-night DMs. Her story unfolded in layers, never in one go. It was always partial, often interrupted but collectively building a picture: raw, magnetic, full of contradiction. She was tender and fierce, soft-spoken and volatile. Her identity was an accumulation of survival and sharp, stubborn dignity.

Sanch's recollections of her life allowed my imagination to make my own story in my head. Her key phrases were always the same: 'My mother was abusive. She screamed at me often, without warning. She was the prettiest woman in her village, or so everyone said. She had schizophrenia but no one called it that and she was never treated. She died when I was sixteen. I've had trouble sitting in the back seat of a car ever since—some combination of panic, memory and motion that I still can't fully explain.'

I tried to imagine Sanch's childhood in a small town in Assam: the house, the smells, the rhythm of life. I pictured her mother, first doting, then increasingly erratic and cruel. Her father, distant but unpredictable. I imagined what it meant to grow up queer, brilliant, angry and aching in that world, to feel suffocated and hyper-aware, to understand violence early on but still believe in revolution.

All the things I imagined Sanch felt, I had felt too. But the roots were different. My parents weren't abusive or mentally ill. My childhood played out in an entirely different realm, one Sanch might have found unfathomable.

And still, somehow, our stories resonated. That stretch, the dissonance and the bridge, is what I'm still trying to understand when I think about my earliest memories.

I thought we were bonded by truth. That our wounds aligned, that the pain meant something.

But we were siphonophores, made of parts that clung to each other for survival, not truth.

We looked like one thing. We weren't that.

And none of it could survive on its own.

I lived in Orlando from age five to ten. There are parts I remember vividly. My mother worked overnight shifts in the neonatal wing of a hospital. My father sold houses by day. We lived in a sprawling brick house in suburban Orlando, with a front yard and garage drive so long, you'd find an excuse not to walk all the way down just to get the mail. There was a netted porch that came before the backyard; it was big enough to rival two neighbourhood parks in Bangalore.

Dozens of creepy stick bugs would cling to the porch net. They were harmless and we got used to them—tiny prehistoric sentinels all around us, protected by the mesh. Sometimes, my brother and I would flick them off. I'd feel terrible afterwards, even though we hadn't really hurt them. They'd fall to the ground and climb right back onto the net.

My parents had achieved what immigrant folklore branded the American Dream. They were Indian, check. They were homeowners, check. But unlike the doctors and engineers who occupied the top tier of the model-minority myth, my parents had taken a different path. My father had earned his broker's licence; my mother requalified as a nurse after migrating. Respectable, stable jobs—yet never quite the pedigreed professions an anxious, caste-polished meritocracy told them they 'should' have reached. It was the late '80s and early '90s, when the Reagan–Bush gospel of meritocracy still felt believable: study hard, work harder and you will win. For a time, it seemed like they had. But the quiet insecurity of not being the 'right kind' of successful never fully left our home. They became the Indians people back home envied, living in homes with central air conditioning and dishwashers, earning more than any generation before them. My father, even in his success, seemed vaguely haunted. His brother was a scientist. He was not. It didn't matter how many houses he sold; he always felt he was outside the circle of prestige.

My mother made good money but at a cost. She gave up her nights to care for other people's fragile babies so she could be present during our days. They were rebels in theory, breaking with tradition when it suited them but still obedient to the deeper codes of caste, success and appearance.

And by 1993, when I was nearly ten, my father made a dramatic choice: we would leave America entirely. The reason? He didn't want us to become 'too American'. And so, we left the land of dreams, only to be claimed by the ghosts we never buried.

Over the next few years in India, some of the most difficult ones of my life (as you can imagine for a child abruptly dropped from the US into a Bangalore school in the '90s), I struggled. I spoke wrong. Ate wrong. Failed miserably in most subjects.

By the time I was a teenager, I began to see the deep fracture my father had carried with him for decades. He yearned for us to succeed on non-traditional terms but his emotional inheritance twisted that desire into something more prescriptive. He wanted us to be respected, not just personally but in the caste-encoded language of prestige.

If his daughter wasn't going to be a doctor or scientist, then she must earn her place in the world with equal weight: a position at the UN, perhaps, or tenure at an elite university. The goal was success and redemption, achieved by alchemizing caste ambition with global class markers.

That fracture was the first time I understood how ideology can camouflage itself as love.

CHAPTER 6

As you know, the last time I saw Sanch was at my place. She was jamming her belongings into her suitcase with the distracted urgency of someone trying to leave more than just a location. The taxi I'd booked was on its way. She wasn't heading back to Hyderabad just yet. First, she was going to Silchar. She wanted to see her extended family, spend time with a cousin she often described as 'the only one who gets me', and, more ominously, finally deal with 'the house'—that vague, looming inheritance mess she'd chronically allude to, ever since her father died in 2021.

We hugged goodbye. I said the usual things people say to blur the edges of a parting: 'Stay safe. Let's talk soon. Come back anytime.' We made loose, hollow plans about the near future. Like one does.

When she left, I felt nothing. No relief, no glowing moment of tenderness. Just an eerie stillness. I wouldn't have admitted it then but now I remember the emptiness like a timestamp.

In our WhatsApp group, Ankur kept the rhythm of Hyderabad going: updates, emoji reactions, the occasional meme drop. I added lazy bits from my life in Bangalore. Sanch sent us photos from Silchar: her hair unusually straight, smiling with a cousin whose face I couldn't place, her slurping Maggi and selfies with Millie, her adopted cat, apparently being taken care of by a housekeeper she had vaguely mentioned once. Some of the voice notes were in Bengali, others in Sylheti, fragments I could still decipher because of the similarities between the two languages.

A few days into the trip, she messaged saying she had a low-grade fever. We told her to go to a doctor, an automatic response friends give, more reflex than care. She went. The next day she told us it was dengue.

There's not much you *can* do about dengue except wait for your body to surrender. The fever, the chills, the surreal ache that burrows into your bones like microscopic parasites, sliding, poking, grazing from the inside. I'd had it once years ago and I can still remember the exhaustion, the strange dreams, the metallic taste of heat. Sanch kept us updated with sarcastic complaints, bedridden selfies and the occasional political rant for flavour.

This is the last memory I have of things being if not normal then at least knowable. Sanch stranded in Silchar with dengue, Ankur in Hyderabad, me in Bangalore. A triangular stasis.

And then, the ground shifted.

Sanch said she was going to the doctor again, this time to get a lump in her breast checked out. Nothing dramatic, she said. Just a routine thing. I expected it to be a cyst.

Within forty-eight hours, it stopped being routine.

She had stage-4 breast cancer. The message dropped like a trapdoor. The report she shared was terrifying in a clinical way: aggressive metastasis, abnormal markers, terrifying sentences strung together in medical jargon. We took turns googling the terms, quietly trying to decode just how bad it really was. And it was bad. We all knew. Even before we said it out loud.

~

Before she was diagnosed with cancer, I'd only heard of Harshvardhan and Urmila in passing. Sanch had mentioned them a couple of times as her OG besties from school days in Silchar. Urmila and she had gone to some protest in Assam and Sanch, like any good far-left activist, carried a proud bruise from being shoved by the police. That story was later confirmed by Urmila once we got talking in a special WhatsApp group set up for Sanch.

Sanch, ever proactive and organized even in the midst of personal crisis, had decided her new friends should be in touch with her old ones—so we could 'cri-cri' together and support each other while digesting the news of her cancer.

'I'll set up the group, make introductions and then leave,' she said. 'I don't want to hear the stuff you guys say about me. I know it's hard to have a friend with cancer but the best support you can give me is by staying connected, letting one person streamline updates. Otherwise, I'll just stress more about you all stressing. I can't deal with that right now.'

She created the group on 26 July 2023, naming it Sanch Support Group. The *Barbie* movie had just been released and she set the display picture to an AI-meme version of Caregiver Barbie. It was funny, irreverent, pure Sanch. If concern, anxiety and worry were side effects of friendship, Sanch would counter them with a mix of stoic humour and razor-sharp pop-culture references.

She claimed her friends seemed more freaked out about the cancer than she was. I gave her the benefit of the doubt. After all, we weren't the ones diagnosed with stage-4 metastasized breast cancer at the age of twenty-seven. Maybe our worry was a cheap pity party and we needed to be cooler than that.

The group was made up of Ankur, my friend Sakshi who is an academic who writes on Dalit feminism, a young doctor I vaguely knew from online spaces, Sanch's childhood friends Urmila and Harshvardhan, and me.

We learned Urmila was in college in Delhi and Harshvardhan had, in Sanch's words, 'sold his soul to corporate' and was working a high-paying job in Mumbai.

'Harsh was always my rich friend,' she once told us. 'His family owns the biggest gold jewellery shop in town. We fight about politics all the time but we're besties. He'd do anything for me.'

That last line gave me a slight twinge of irritation; she knew Ankur would read it. But maybe I was projecting. Maybe I was confusing the sacred legacy of long-term friendship with a slightly underhanded dig at Ankur, who had empty pockets and was still studying for a government exam.

Ankur, already a walking worst-case-scenario machine, now faced a reality worse than any he'd imagined. The one person who had taught him that life could be light, joyful, even silly, was most likely going to be very sick for the next few years. This was the best case. And the worst case …

For once, he came to the group with a concrete plan. As long as Sanch was in Silchar, he said, he wanted to make sure one of us was always with her. He'd go first.

But in our regular WhatsApp group comprising Sanch, Ankur and me, Sanch's updates started off vague, like suggestions, then quickly shifted into instructions.

'No no, chill, Urmila and Harshvardhan are going to be here on 5 August. They'll stay awhile. After that, you guys can think about coming.'

Minutes later, as if on cue, Urmila chimed in on the support group: 'Ankur, don't worry, I'll be there on 5 August to stay with Sanch. Harshvardhan will come soon after.'

I remember feeling grateful. I typed back: 'So great Sanch has such wonderful friends.'

But then I asked the practical question: wasn't Urmila in college? Semester break or not, she'd have to return in a few weeks, right?

Ankur replied right after: 'Yeah, so I can book my ticket when you need to head back to Delhi.'

Urmila's response was calm: 'Don't worry. I'm not going back this semester. What matters right now is Sanch. I'll be with her for however long it takes.'

I pushed again. 'But what about your degree? You can't do this alone. It's going to take a community.'

Minutes later, she replied: 'What is a college semester when it comes to Sanch? I can make it up later.'

Then Harshvardhan entered the chat: 'Don't worry, I'm getting permission to work from Silchar for at least four months. I'll be there to help Urmila.'

Urmila: 'Are you sure work will be okay with that?'

Harshvardhan: 'Yeah, I applied for six months of remote work. I'll drop a few projects but my boss is cool with it.'

Something twisted in my gut. A swirl of nausea. Worry, but also something else, for Ankur. Why wasn't he pushing back? Why wasn't he saying, no matter what their offerings were, he'd be with Sanch too? He loved her. Shouldn't he be the one there?

But the tone had already been set. Sure, we *could* visit. But first, we had to wait till Urmila and Harsh got there to handle things.

And the same reason Ankur wasn't confidently saying he'd go anyway was why I wasn't booking a flight immediately, even if just for a weekend.

People say you can't read tone over text. That it's easy to misinterpret. But I could read between the lines. There was something orchestrated in Urmila's and Harshvardhan's messages, no matter how casual they sounded. It was like they were saying:

> We'll set the rules.
> Sanch is our person.
> This is our operation.
> You're welcome to support.
> But you don't get to lead.

Only a year later, Ankur recounted how Sanch had crumbled his already half-existing confidence in himself in the months before cancer, the time when things were supposed to be good. At home, it looked ordinary: movies, video games, nights that passed quietly. But Sanch had a habit—she needed to know everything in advance. Endings, twists, trivia. Even cheat codes to video games they played. She'd read them all before watching. Ankur asked for no spoilers. A small request. But she never stopped.

When he protested, Sanch turned it into judgment. 'Really? That's what you're sad about? A spoiler? Compared to everything happening in the world?'

Or sometimes she'd pout, 'You made me feel bad about giving you a spoiler—you don't believe me. I figured things out on my own, I am sorry I always ruin it for you, it's not my fault the stuff you enjoy is so predictable and boring and dumb and I am so smart.'

He learned to swallow it and, eventually, to apologize. 'You made me feel bad for giving you a spoiler,' she'd say until he accepted his guilt. Only once, when he snapped, did she stop. She seemed to know then she'd finally touched something he wouldn't bend.

The roommate added another layer of pressure. They told Sanch: 'If you wanted to transition, would Ankur still love you?' Sanch had no plans to transition but she repeated the question anyway. When Ankur tried to answer honestly, 'I can't know until that moment comes,' it became a verdict: he was transphobic. His support for trans rights had never just been rhetoric. Yes, he argued online, cut ties with friends who were hostile or bigoted. But it was also evident in the quieter, material things, like finding housing where his roommate would feel safe, pooling money when someone in the community needed it. His solidarity wasn't a performance; it was the texture of his everyday life, including the effort he took over the years to educate and change his mind about so many issues the average small-town Indian boy should have been bigoted about.

Other betrayals came quieter. Sanch and the roommate planned to rent a place together, not telling him until he stumbled across it. When he confronted them, they brushed it aside. She had already been weighing whom to keep and whom to cut, depending on what served her next move.

It was in small things too. She'd laugh at something she was reading, then refuse to tell him why. When he said it made him feel shut out, she promised she'd stop but never did. She inserted herself into his friendships, found ways to play the victim or painted a friend as suspect on identity-politics grounds. The pressure was clear: if he didn't end the friendship, he wasn't just neglecting her, he was failing her and the roommate too.

The shifts could be absurd. Once, she sneezed ten times in a row and he teased her gently. She turned sharp, the roommate backing her up. Another time, mid-dinner, she snapped at nothing, face turning cold, superior. His whole body learned to panic then, scrambling to coax her back to the version of Sanch he knew, instead of facing who she was in those moments.

When she got sick, he was never allowed near. At the PG, it was always an excuse: 'The landlady is a bigot, I don't want anyone around when I'm unwell.' If he dropped her off at college, she insisted he leave her a hundred metres from the gate. 'No one should see us together,' she said. His reality bent around her requests until it barely resembled his own.

By then, he admitted, he was scared of her. Isolation had thickened around him, the kind that doesn't look like what it is at first. It looks like compromise, like privacy, like the natural give-and-take of intimacy. But slowly it rearranges your sense of what's real. He began to believe this might just be normal. This might just be what love was supposed to feel like.

So, when the cancer arrived, he didn't question the barriers. Of course, he wanted to fly down. But there were always reasons. A friend said the timing was impossible. Sanch said he wouldn't understand the language, the food, the place. She had no bandwidth, she said, to manage him too.

None of it made sense. But by then, sense was no longer the point.

~

When Sanch first told us about the cancer and shared her reports, our reactions were a tangled mess of frantic texts, panicked voice notes, morbid memes and general existential chaos.

After getting off my phone, I burst into tears and wandered aimlessly to my favourite coffee shop. It was a work-from-home day, which often meant an excuse to haunt Third

Wave Coffee and pretend to be productive. That day, though, I stared at my laptop like it had personally offended me. I clicked through inboxes and websites out of muscle memory. I was doing branding for a fintech company at the time, crafting core messaging for an audience that now felt utterly fictional. Eventually, I surrendered and fell down a YouTube rabbit hole, looking up cancer survivors, stage-4 diagnoses, living while dying, terminal illness TikToks. Anything the algorithm slung at me after I typed 'cancer'.

Then someone I knew walked into the cafe. Sheila was a mother of three with a business and a chronic lack of free time, so I didn't expect her to be one of the first people to offer me comfort. But she spotted me, came over, rubbed my hand and asked gently, 'Are you okay?' I promptly dissolved into tears again.

'My friend ... she's only twenty-seven. She just got diagnosed with stage-4 breast cancer.'

Sheila hugged me and said, 'That totally, utterly sucks.' She offered to walk with me. We crossed Indiranagar's chaotic main road and slipped into its hushed, tree-lined inner lanes.

I don't remember what we talked about but I remember the moment I realized something: Sanch's story was going to ripple into lives far beyond her own. Her diagnosis had yanked mortality out of the abstract and shoved it into our bones. I was nearly twelve years older than her. I had twelve more cancer-free years than her. And the guilt of that started to feel like a tax I hadn't paid.

Survivor's guilt is the most illogical currency of grief. Or maybe it's just a narcissistic ledger. Constant, silent comparisons between those who suffer and those who merely spectate. Maybe it's grief's most self-absorbed shadow.

A few days later, Urmila texted to say that Sanch was deeply attached to her hometown, Silchar. That she'd want to be rooted somewhere familiar, even if that place carried the residue of a difficult past. Ankur and I felt like jackasses. Maybe our lists of the best cancer centres in India were too much. The internet swelled with well-meaning strangers offering her housing in Delhi, Mumbai, Bangalore. But try imagining you're twenty-seven, ill, terrified and suddenly expected to heal in the spare room of a stranger's flat. Faced with a life-altering diagnosis, her decision made sense. Aching sense.

I put myself in her shoes. Even the kindest host can feel like a burden when your life is disintegrating. Sanch had every right to hold on to her autonomy. Her body, her disease, her terms.

So, we waited. We went back to sending memes, trading bleak cancer jokes and letting her come to us when she wanted.

I texted: 'You have every right to stay in Silchar. We didn't mean to overwhelm you. Take your time. We'll wait until you've had a chance to process before we come visit.'

Sanch replied: 'Thanks bestie, that's all I needed to hear from you.'

Around that time, I introduced Sanch to my friend Aparupa Gupta on WhatsApp. Aparupa and I had worked together since 2014. By day she was an accountant, by night a magnetic performer. She sang ghazals with aching grace, belted out pop and Bollywood anthems and could resurrect the soul of Nina Simone in a smoky bar.

Back in 2014, while I was working with her, Aparupa was diagnosed with breast cancer when she was only twenty-five years old. Chemotherapy came in waves. Her hair disappeared, menopause came early, her skin cracked, her face hollowed. But she survived. She was in remission and had just celebrated ten years of being cancer-free. Her joy shone through her grin but her body still whispered her story through fatigue, long silences and flashes of doubt.

When I heard about Sanch, I had instinctively messaged Aparupa. She replied immediately: 'Send me her number.'

A day later, Sanch texted to say how incredible Aparupa was. How freeing it felt to swap stories, compare notes and finally talk to someone who *got it.* Their chats became their own orbit. I imagined them trading lists of meds and side effects and tactics for clinging to a sense of self.

I started spiralling deeper into Reddit cancer forums. Some for patients, some for the collateral damage (read: us, the watchers). Every post felt like a Lego block in the weird castle I was building in my head. The stories were from everywhere. Stories that screamed one thing: cancer is hell. It's chaos, random, merciless and entirely un-universal. And nothing I read in those American-heavy forums mapped neatly on to a twenty-seven-year-old woman in Silchar, without a mother or father. With only a handful of indifferent relatives who drove her to appointments and nothing more.

Then came the update. Sanch had found one of the top doctors in Assam. A man who'd returned from overseas oncology programmes to set up a cancer institute in his hometown. I did my stalking. I was impressed. We had a moment of reckoning. Sanch, Ankur and I had all deeply internalized the cult of city hospitals. The glimmering floors, the robotic voice announcements, the glass-and-chrome temples of modern medicine. But maybe the best doctor is the one who came back. Who stayed rooted. Who wanted to make healthcare work without bankrupting people.

Sanch was counterculture. And deep down, we wanted to be, too. Even as we obsessively reread her report and tried to understand her prognosis by mashing together peer-reviewed journals, Reddit threads and whatever Google spat out. In my mind, she had a year. Maybe five. But with pain, lots of it.

We built our own messed-up formula: Denial + Despair ÷ Hope x Internet = Grief Math.

It never really added up.

CHAPTER 7

May 2025

Utsav stood behind the badminton net, doing a silly victory dance and baiting me with mock aggression. His face was a rapid montage of gleeful expressions, part taunting, part goofy. I had 2 points to his 9. In the last few months of writing this book, we'd taken up playing badminton at one of the many neighbourhood sports centres that have mushroomed all over Bangalore, another hyper-local spawn of the city's startup metabolism.

'Suck this,' I yelled, swinging my racquet in a violent, doomed arc. Utsav rushed up to the net, bent low and coolly shot the shuttlecock right back at me.

Utsav and I have been married for four years. We're a pandemic couple who met on Bumble. I had missed the entire dating-app era because I was either married or in a long-term relationship when apps became the norm. At thirty-six, single again (albeit briefly, I don't do long stints in singlehood), I decided to finally explore it. I'm a serial monogamist, though my history with marriage has been … complicated.

I once saw a tweet that said, 'No one in their twenties should get married, you don't know who you are yet. But if you're divorced before thirty, you're a legend.'

I cackled. Because here's the truth: not only was I divorced by thirty, I was divorced *twice.* For an Indian woman, that's an Olympic-level performance. Thankfully, I didn't get pregnant during either marriage. Both marriages were just very different responses to unresolved childhood trauma. I know, groundbreaking.

When my second marriage ended when I was twenty-nine, I swore I'd never marry again. I envisioned long-term live-in relationships, romantic bohemia with a side of Bollywood. After my first two marriages, I had a long relationship that lasted eight years. It gave me space to find my voice and confidence in my career. It was optimistic, sweetly symbiotic. We split in 2020.

I only met Utsav because I realized I had a window to try dating apps. I joined Bumble like an excited kid. The first few profiles were duds, men posing beside luxury cars or describing themselves as 'politically neutral' like it was a flex. Then came Utsav. No bells and whistles. Just a kind face, curly hair, with an adopted Indie dog and a reading habit. His profile had humble brags (he spoke French) and he seemed to be, at least on paper, genuinely progressive. We chatted for five hours. I asked to meet him almost immediately.

I'm impulsive like that. Sometimes, it leads to magic. Sometimes, to temporary social obliteration. Utsav was surprised by my invitation to meet within forty-eight hours of us talking but he agreed. We met at Blue Tokai in late

August 2020. He showed up in a full-face shield. I teased him. 'My dad's elderly,' he said. 'I need to be careful.' I nodded in quick, embarrassed support.

When we sat down, he replaced the shield with a regular mask. I exhaled. He had a slight lisp and a very Bangalore accent. We traded life facts. What struck me most was how unbothered he was by my past. He was thirty-three years old, younger than me but unfazed by my divorces or the winding paths I'd taken. He had brought a copy of my book *The Body Myth* for me to sign. 'What a suck-up,' I teased. He smiled.

Utsav didn't fit the cis-het archetype I'd grown accustomed to. He embodied his values. He wasn't hung up on labels or judgment. What mattered to him was intent. Sure, he was awkward and sometimes uncertain but he had a genuine presence that made me feel deeply seen. Our dating phase wasn't smooth. Utsav was struggling with intense, episodic depression when we met.

We survived his emotional shutdowns with patience, conversation and slow trust-building. I learned not to take his silences personally. Early into our dating, I sent him an essay, something creative and deeply weird, because that's who I am. All these years later, he's still okay with me sharing excerpts from that letter.

October 2020

Subject: An Imaginary Essay for Utsav

It's Monday night and I am stalking Utsav on Instagram. I've obviously got a lot more free time than he does and

I make the most of it. As I am going through the familiar motions of stalking a new love interest, something profoundly unfamiliar happens. It starts to feel futile in comparison to the mental notes I've already made of him in his physical presence. Stalking has never felt futile before. This is new.

For the record, I've never written an essay on a boyfriend. Even though I've been writing about everything ever since I can remember. But Utsav in my life, at this time, demands something almost hagiographical in nature. Not to romanticize him. The devotional part here comes from the potent life reflections (and some unadulterated joy) that come at me rapidly in the weeks I've known him.

In these weeks of knowing him, all sense of decorum has already gone out the window. I've emotionally vomited on him multiple times in a span of time most people would call brief. Like the real hardcore kind of vomit, lumpy undigested bits too. He's the man, taking it with a bulletproof vest and all. If he thinks I am complete batshit, he's not letting it on. Either out of courtesy, goodwill or the slight chance he knows it's the good kind of batshit.

He's silently inching towards my vomit spills, inspecting for clarity, truth, making sure there is no bullshit-induced spillage.

I'd like to start out on the defence here. I think we go through the stalking route because we're trying to find how our past dovetailed into our present. Did I say we? I meant I. But also, in general, people. People stalk to find the speckles of a human that potentially could mean so much to them. People stalk to pull out the shards of glass, the ones that cut you when you realize that till a point, this person was a stranger to you.

I want to know what he thought about in 2013 and what he was obsessed about in 1999. I want to read comments he wrote under ubiquitous posts in 2017. What song was stuck in your head in 2012, Utsav?

Some of this becomes immaterial because I found something in him that's very much made up of the same essence. I can't put a name to it, it will remain a mystical construct. Some energy that experienced the world with the same lens. Something like that. Something achingly beautiful like that.

Lately, he's been telling me stories about his past with details that pop from his voice into a movie screen in my head. His details are vivid, I can smell it, see it and remember it days later.

Like the Bournvita his father made when he was a child in Delhi. In winter. And all I see is the froth of the Bournvita bubbles on top in a glass waiting to be drunk. I see a spoon *kat-kat-kat*-ing frantically, rising to the static coldness in the air, till the froth becomes thick enough for his specific liking.

These borrowed visions have become richer to me than any result of stalking. I've never met a person who has been so abundant with thought and tenderness. It's supplemented by a raw, almost rabid, appreciation for the existential treadmill we're on.

He appears to be too humble. He's accomplished things few can, he thinks about things in fragments that most can't even fathom. In his free time, I think he is a map-preparer. He prepares maps of the dark tunnels he's willing to walk into, fights those inevitable monsters out of choice. He knows his darkness well, there are parts of our entire human collective that reside in him. Our memories in his. Our doings in his.

It's hard to take accountability for the rancid nature of our collective worst qualities. And then there are a very rare few, like Utsav, who take it up like a sport.

Some of us do that mostly to fill holes in ourselves, to distract ourselves with pain so we have stories to tell others or to perform.

He does it because it's a part of his existence. To not go into them would be a life unlived. This is what I know about him with sureness. It's a brave existence. One that allows him to offer straight-shooter vibes with such potent tenderness. His magic trick is his unawareness of how powerfully needed he is in our world. His folly is not seeing how he subverts every little toxic pebble thrown at him and makes something unexpectedly tremendous with it.

His folly is not understanding that I could see all this in less than a month. He is unaware of why it's easy to see him—he has built himself in a mesmerizing makes-no-real-sense shape in a world where everyone's still trying to develop unsustainable, rigid shapes from cookie-cutter manuals they can't even comprehend.

Or maybe it's not his folly. Just his way of expanding into an unlikely pose in an unlikable world. A considered stance that must make it hard to breathe sometimes, one he still refuses to move out of. Anything less would be unoriginal. Unfathomable.

I started with stalking, with the desire to stalk, the desire to obsess. Instead, I am writing this. I don't want to admit stalking defeat just yet but what it appears to be is something of a paradox.

Utsav isn't a person who is stalkable. You can't stalk a person who carries his mysteries so self-assuredly on his back, inside his chest, tangled in his head. You can't stalk a person who holds multiple subtitles for every sentence, without any agenda to misinterpret. He's talking to you with subtext and a context that can keep changing but never lacks in its authenticity to express. When he speaks, you'll see some cosmic irony come undone.

His slow sentences are cynical of routed ideas. His presence is an act of rerouting. He's not as cynical as he thinks he is. It's a coping mechanism, insurance for oxygen, it's the conscious act of opening a few stitches in his shirt allowing him potential to exhale through the parts of his life that threaten to choke him.

But most of all, what all of this gives me is, ironically, the ability to breathe again. Without thinking if there's enough air for me in the long run. Deep, satiating breaths that I know I won't run out of. These breaths come with awe. Because I now see it's possible for people like him to exist. What swallows me whole is the other truth. The other side of this paradox.

The cost of a miracle is what it has sustained in order to be one.

If one is to witness him, just to feel a fleeting moment of relief, then you'll have to count how many full breaths he's given up to be him. I'll have to count how many agonized life circumstances he's had to counter with his spine. How many subversions he's had to calculate to resist the urge to fall into what every other man I've met before had to fall into.

Counting them won't make up for the bursts of suffocation he's experienced. It won't grant him a get-out-jail-free card for all that's been endured to be him. I know the world we've lived in and I know the layers one must reconstruct to make it bearable on some days. I know the grief that comes with going incognito for spans of time, just so that no one suspects you are being something radically opposite to what your environment told you to be. But it will make him a miracle.

Instead of stalking, I am counting. Each suffocation of the past that's allowed him to bloom sideways, through the cracks. I am counting the ones in the future that will still threaten to splinter the spine that's held up till now. I am counting in the hope that sometime, soon, the ease of breath he's offered me expands right into the sky till it's no longer discernible. In the hope that he breathes it right in and, for a brief moment, realizes he's never owed anything else except himself to this fractured world we've both existed in.

~

We got married in a courthouse just eleven months after I sent him this essay in an email. Over the years, we laid bare our hypocrisies, internalized narratives and the shame we'd both carried. A year into our marriage, Utsav confided something deeper: caste trauma.

His father was Dalit. His mother, Brahmin. It was a marriage of convenience. His father was sixteen years older than his mother. Utsav was born into an arrangement shaped more by necessity than compatibility and he spent much of his life masking aspects of his identity.

'Anonymity,' he told me one night. 'That's what caste trauma has felt like. Like I was living in hiding. I tried to blend in, read what the savarnas read, talk like them, but I always knew I didn't fully belong. You're vocally anti-caste and some of your DBA [Dalit-Bahujan-Adivasi] friends talk about it openly. But I think most inter-caste or marginalized people aren't emotionally equipped to do that. There's too much shame.'

Up until that point, I had assumed my own identity complexities had shaped my experience in layered ways. But this was a deeper wound. An interfaith marriage might be legible to mainstream discourse. Caste? It's a quieter devastation. It tells you that you don't belong before you even understand what belonging is.

We accepted each other's experiences. We navigated the frictions. And we found the beauty and the maddening ordinariness of a modern urban marriage in upper-middle-class Bangalore.

By the time Utsav and I were married, I had started to become more aware of Sanch online. We had been engaging with each other a month after our our initial fundraiser-DM meet-cute and I had been tracking her political stances that ranged from the intricacies of Assam's social history to animal rights and trans rights.

I can't remember exactly when I first told Utsav about Sanch but it must have been a bit before her first visit. Utsav has this implicit trust in anyone I call home. If someone mattered to me, that was enough. He would do whatever it took to be the perfect host.

The only inkling Utsav had about who Sanch really was came during her first visit to our house. We were out on the balcony smoking cigarettes, tossing around mildly pretentious opinions on random topics. The conversation eventually gathered momentum and landed on communism.

Utsav, bless him, launched into the distinctions between different types of communism. For the sake of your sanity, dearest reader, I'll skip the deep dive. But this is what stuck: Sanch didn't lean in. She stiffened.

She had already declared herself a 'fierce communist' but when Utsav gently brought up anarcho-communism (thanks, Utsav), instead of expanding the conversation, talking about luxury communism, libertarian communism, religious variants, hell, even just Marxist basics, she froze.

She said, simply, 'I'm just a Marxist.'

Now, that answer would've been fine, if not for the lip quiver. A visible tremble, like she might cry if the topic continued. The energy shifted. The air felt charged. Her defensiveness buzzed and thickened around us.

Had Utsav's unintentional lecture triggered something? Was her understanding more fragile than we thought? I had always assumed she was better read than both Utsav and I combined. That belief came from seeing her post long, thoughtful Instagram stories: full of radical resonance, political fire and emotional intelligence. Clearly, I'd filled in the blanks. I'd imagined her finishing whole books before posting those stories. Now, I wasn't so sure.

Utsav, who usually takes a few extra minutes to read a room, noticed something too. Gently, he asked, 'What does being a Marxist mean to you?'

The silence that followed was drought-dry. Sanch's tone went stiff. Almost performative. 'I *am* a Marxist,' she repeated.

We didn't know what to say. I'm sure I tried to defuse the moment with a joke or a distraction. Sanch slowly stood up and walked downstairs to the living room.

A few minutes later, I followed. She sat there with a half-pout, her energy tight, her gaze darting.

When she saw me, she looked momentarily uncomfortable. Then she spotted Jeera on the other couch and pivoted, quickly, loudly.

'Jeeru-Jeeru, Jeeru-Jeeru!'

Jeera perked his ears slightly, looked at her with tepid interest and stayed seated. That was enough. She had reset her emotional state like she'd just changed the channel.

I asked if she wanted coffee. She nodded. We melted into a new mood, as if nothing had happened. Communism was over. Dinner plans resumed. The glitch was smoothed over like a bad edit.

Later that night, in bed, Utsav turned to me.

'That was weird. Did I offend her?' he asked.

'No, you didn't. That *was* weird.'

Then we went to sleep.

What he didn't know then was that was the least bizarre thing he'd confront and have to live through just a year later. In a year, he'd become the one responding to messages when I was buried under pillows, caught in the tug-of-war between my need to be publicly transparent and the relentless pitchfork curiosity of the Instagram janta. People who thought they were entitled to the whole story. People who attacked the messenger.

But that was only the start. Utsav would be the one holding the broken, mentally scrambled pieces of me through the entirety of 2024. The aftershocks of the Sanch scam hit hardest a few months after I went public. My depression deepened. The paralysis set in. Utsav stood beside me as I tried experimental, cutting-edge treatments. He stayed with me in the same room at the psychiatric hospital I inevitably landed in by September 2024.

Here's what I learned: trauma doesn't respond to chaos. It waits. It sits. It curls in the corners until the drama fades, until the vultures leave. Only then does it stretch itself out inside you. Only then does your body start leaking the truth. And when it does, the pain comes from nowhere.

Being a victim has never been my identity. Being a foolish one? Even harder to swallow. But there I was. Listless. Blank. Unable to imagine a way out of the ache that came from such a fantastical emotional and financial betrayal.

CHAPTER 8

Before the meds, the radiation or the surgery, there was the fundraiser.

Very soon after Urmila's hard boundaries were laid out, clear instructions that we shouldn't come to Silchar, we tried to pivot. We flooded Sanch with support in other ways. Reddit stories about cancer. Dark memes. Silly jokes. Anything that might make her laugh.

Then the tone shifted.

In the group chat that included Urmila, Harshvardhan, Ankur, me, an academic and a young doctor friend, Urmila suddenly said something different: 'When you come to Silchar, we'll take care of you guys. Host you end to end. You won't have to worry about a thing. We just need to set things up first.'

It felt like emotional whiplash. First, we were told not to come. Now, we were being promised a hero's welcome. Still, we took it as a positive turn. Maybe Sanch was feeling better. Maybe she was softening.

That's when the fundraiser conversation started.

In our smaller group of Ankur, Sanch and me, Sanch was adamant. 'Under no circumstances will you guys do a public fundraiser for me,' she said. 'I'm a Dalit/Adivasi kid. Everyone out there wants to believe we're grifters. People will say cruel things. Even if some are kind, I can't deal with trolls right now.'

It was clear. No fundraiser.

But in the bigger group, after Ankur and I mentioned her refusal, the energy flipped again. We were talking about other logistics when Urmila messaged me directly: 'Rheea, she will HAVE to do a fundraiser. I know her family situation very well. She's too humble to ask but she needs it.'

I panicked. If this was what she needed, we had to do it. I messaged back immediately: 'Then we'll do it! Let's get it going. Should we use Milaap [a fundraising platform]?'

Our academic friend suggested Instagram but emphasized the need for a legit platform. That's when Urmila said, 'No, not Milaap. They're anti-trans. We've had issues getting money from them. I can't tell you how much mutual aid got stuck because of these biased platforms.'

I take full accountability here, I was swayed. Swayed by the invocation of marginalization. The weaponization of identity. It bypassed my instincts. If Milaap was problematic, I didn't want to perpetuate harm.

'Cool,' I said. 'Then I'll write the best fundraiser appeal ever.'

We made a plan. The money would go into Ankur's account for transparency. He would disburse it to Sanch based on the bills she provided. We would provide documents and expenses to anyone who asked. We thought we were building a system that was both compassionate and accountable. We detailed everything in the fundraiser that was a mix of irreverent Sanch and our general kooky vibe—yes, even for a cancer fundraiser.

The post was a series of slides. The first slide had an arrow pointing at a picture of Sanch, who was wearing loud pink and blue eyeshadow. It simply said: 'This is Sanch.' The second slide told people about her being a freelancer, along with her identities and all the work she had done for the community in education and fundraising. And then the heartstopper, that she was diagnosed with stage-4 cancer. We included pictures of her reports and mentioned all the details about it going to Ankur's account so he could give her the funds as she needed it for treatment. There were a lot of things she needed already: thoracentesis, hormone blockers, lumpectomy, then radiation. We promised regular updates, public documentation and pauses between disbursements. We thought we were building trust. Instead, we were unknowingly writing a manifesto of credibility for someone who never intended to honour any of it.

The response was overwhelming. In less than forty-eight hours, the fundraiser had crossed four lakh rupees. The post caught fire—1,800 likes, nearly 100 comments, dozens of shares. The visuals were bold, the copy had bite and the diagnosis was backed up with screenshot snippets from medical reports.

There was the Barbie vs. Oppenheimer meme, which I captioned 'Sanch two weeks ago/Sanch today'. There was the hook: 'That's Sanch. Their story went from bad to ... really really bad.' I'd written it half in grief, half in hustle mode, believing with every cell that we were doing something urgent, real and right. And more than anything, I thought I was giving Sanch the best gift I could, not some sad tragic fundraiser but a Sanch cancer fundraiser that captured her ironic sense of humour and appetite to be irreverent.

And it worked. People responded. Donations poured in from India, the diaspora, even folks I hadn't spoken to in years. We were crying at our phones, sending voice notes back and forth, stunned by the kindness we'd received. We were doing something good.

My friend Vani Subramanian, a narrative-based therapist, a person with equal measures of humour and grief, sent the post to all her international friends and even managed to get people to donate from abroad. I didn't know it then but the credibility of networks I had built over decades was about to be crumbled under the weight of one human. Vani, who didn't even know of Sanch, asked me if she could send a care package to Assam for her. Such was the type of goodness Sanch attracted with her story.

But within three days of the fundraiser, Sanch panicked. She messaged us saying that too many people were DMing her. Too many questions. 'I'm not ready to be this visible,' she wrote. 'I feel paranoid. Please take it down.'

So, we did. We archived the post. Just like that, it was gone. And no public update followed. Sanch put up a few stories thanking everyone, nothing too over the top, nothing too emotional, Sanch just being Sanch. But it seemed she had made an impact. Writers, artists, activists, ex-colleagues and complete strangers who resonated with her story all wanted to help, give money and spread the word. It was one of those moments that made you believe in people again. When community feels like a real, breathing organism.

Sanch messaged me tearfully after we crossed ₹4.5 lakh. 'I don't know how to thank you,' she said. 'This is saving my life.'

We were thrilled. Touched. Deeply emotional. We cried while sending updates to each other. We watched the counter tick upwards and felt a real sense of purpose. We were helping someone fight cancer. We were doing something good.

But it was also the first time Sanch's cancer stopped being just her story. It became a public one. One where money and accountability entered the picture. One where hundreds of people now had a stake in her survival.

Within a week she told us she was starting on medications. It started with Paclitaxel (Taxol). Sanch told us that it was the oral chemo she was on. Aparupa confirmed it was standard; she'd been on it herself. It's often used in hormone receptor-positive breast cancer cases. That seemed to check out. A few weeks later came the first updates about radiation therapy. Short, slightly dramatic voice notes. Some Instagram stories with vague captions. There was even one image of a radiation room that she claimed was from her hospital. We held on to every crumb, our eyes hungry for proof and proximity.

A month later came the surgery.

A lump removal, she told us. We all wanted to be there. Mostly, I wanted Ankur to be there. And Ankur wanted to be there more than anyone. She went back to her usual list of reasons for why he couldn't come. He could not speak the language, and the food would be too difficult for him to adapt to.

It was, to put it mildly, ridiculous. The first flag raised in my subconscious there but it wasn't red, only a mild shade of pink.

She wasn't in another country. She was in Silchar. He spoke Hindi. Millions of people navigate dietary surprises every day. But Sanch had a way of warping reality to suit her emotional staging. Ankur was left confused, doubting himself, constantly questioning his own reactions. He felt gaslit and we, caught in the glowing fog of her narrative, let it happen.

Harshvardhan sent voice notes after the surgery. 'She's loopy from the anaesthesia,' he said. 'She's having imaginary conversations with her dad. Asking nurses for selfies.'

We thought it was cute. Classic Sanch. Even under sedation, still bold, still playing with the boundaries of social decorum. But something didn't sit right. She was a selfie queen and we only got one picture. A sterile white bed. No IV, no tubes, no bruising, no messy post-op moment. Just a curated still life of Sanch-in-bed.

No one said it out loud but I remember the silence in our WhatsApp group the day after. We were trying to believe her. Trying to trust that one image was enough. But this was a woman who took fifty pictures just to show off her cup of chai.

In the weeks after the surgery, Harshvardhan became more visible as her caretaker. Sanch messaged one evening to say he'd bought her a brand-new laptop, 'So I can start applying for jobs again,' she wrote. She was elated. She even sent a picture of it. At the time, it felt like a beautiful gesture. Harsh came from money. He had a well-paying job in Mumbai. Of course he'd get his best friend with stage-4 cancer a laptop. We didn't think twice about it.

A couple of weeks later came more news. She said she wanted to go to Delhi to study—to feel alive again, to reimagine her life beyond cancer. It felt noble. Radical. Romantic, even. Ankur, who had always wanted to be with her physically, finally had a real chance to see her. Delhi wasn't far. In fact, it was far easier to get a direct flight to Delhi than it was to Silchar. There were no logistical barriers.

He asked her, gently, if he could visit. Her response was evasive and emotionally loaded.

> Ankur: 'Let me come for the weekend. I can be in Delhi by Friday.'
>
> Sanch: 'You're trying to make my illness about you.'
>
> Ankur: 'I am sorry baby, I just want to be with you.'
>
> Sanch: 'Help looks like listening, not barging into a vulnerable space.'
>
> Ankur: 'I am not trying to intrude, just understand, be with you …'
>
> Sanch: 'Why does everything I say get turned into a negotiation?'
>
> Ankur: 'Bebee, I love you, I wish you were here with me. I am sorry, I'll give you space.'

Sanch: 'Thanks baby. Could send me 2,500 for medications? I low on medical funds.'

Ankur: 'Sure. Done.'

Sanch: 'I am sorry bebee, I keep asking for money, you must hate me.'

Ankur: 'No! I just want to be able to come and take care of you.'

Every time Ankur asked a question, she reframed it as him being controlling. Concern became coercion. Distance became intimacy but on her terms. There was no stable self, only a series of curated identities that flared up when challenged and dissolved when accountability came knocking. He backed off. Apologized. Internalized it. And then days later, she messaged him asking for money. That's when I saw Ankur begin to emotionally unravel. Slowly. Quietly. But unmistakably.

Then came a call from Aparupa.

It was abrupt. It seemed she'd been holding something back for weeks.

'Rheea,' she said, her voice taut, 'I'll go to hell for saying this if I'm wrong. But I have to say it, it's not adding up. She told me she's taking the same meds I was on. And look, I'm not saying all cancer patients react the same way, I really, really know they don't. But there's no way she looks that healthy. Months into treatment, her skin is glowing. I mean, listen, I feel terrible even saying this. I could be wrong and I'll happily burn in hell if I am but just ... watch out. Please.'

I remember freezing.

I said something like, 'Yeah ... some weird things have been adding up,' and promised to keep an eye out. That night, I began to look at Sanch with new eyes. Not with certainty, not with suspicion, just a soft recalibration. A willingness to see something I had previously blocked out.

I didn't think she was lying about having cancer. That felt impossible to even consider. But I did start to wonder if she was lying about treating it. About Delhi. About what the hell she was really doing there.

And maybe that's what made it easier to stay in denial, because how can you accuse someone of faking cancer? How do you even begin to hold that thought without choking on it?

But the very next day, Aparupa, riddled with guilt for even admitting to me that she suspected Sanch might not be as ill as she claimed, called her to talk about medications. Then, Aparupa called me.

'Rheea! So, I talked to Sanch, they stopped that medication, so she's only been on radiation now. She is taking a break, so I jumped to conclusions. If she's been off the med for a month, she probably would feel and look a lot healthier.'

I felt relief but by the time I put the phone down I felt unease. I felt Aparupa switching this hard was unlike her. She had come to me with a risky confession and her own guilt made her call Sanch up to make sure she wasn't imagining things. But that's the thing ... it dawned on me, whatever question you ask Sanch, especially if it is a follow-up, you are met with an easy answer, an almost obvious one. The kind of answer that stopped you from asking for more elaborate details. Aparupa was convinced for that day. In the next few weeks, we'd realize, both of us no longer felt at ease with her answer.

That week, I pulled up an essay I wrote years ago that was published on the wonderful but now-defunct feminist website The Ladies Finger. It was about my first marriage. The one that had gone viral on Facebook. The one Utsav had read when we first started dating. I had sent it to Sanch too, back when she was still new in my life. Back when she said she wanted to know everything about me.

'I got married when I was 20 because I was homesick ...'

That's how it started. With my foolish, soft-bellied truth. I reread the whole thing. The humiliation. The detachment. The yearning to belong. The good-girl conditioning. The buried anger.

It hit me that my trauma had been an open source. I'd handed Sanch my past in a beautifully written, emotionally vulnerable document. And now I couldn't tell whether she had studied it or absorbed it. Mirrored it or mimicked it.

But the thing about truth is, it never gives you what you want. It gives you what you need.

That essay wasn't closure. It was a rupture. A public gutting. I wrote it with one eye open, terrified that the world would think I was either pathetic or performative. I was scared of sounding like I hadn't moved on. I was scared of sounding like I had.

> Shame can shift shapes. Sometimes, it performs as modesty. Sometimes, it appears as a virtue. But mostly, it keeps you quiet.

Sanch and I had conversations about shame and its role in silence and in social justice. I now believe she misunderstood what I meant entirely. She thought I was confessing a weakness. She didn't see it for what it really was: a middle finger dipped in grace.

Yes, she took my trauma as a script. Yes, she used my emotional blueprint to choreograph sympathy. She thought the shame and embarrassment of being scammed by a young woman like her would keep me quiet, petrified for my reputation. She thought I was someone who would edit my story with cheap cosmetics and lies to come out looking okay. Sanch's Panglossian expectations missed the most important part of my emotional survival. I moved on. I didn't get stuck in shame or pity or endless edits of my own pain. I got free. I grew. I laughed about it. I built things. I paid taxes. I danced in kitchens and wrote my heart out. I tried a different kind of therapy. I was moving towards healing. She was running exactly the opposite way.

Sanch calculated for attention. She calculated for protection. She even calculated for applause. But she didn't calculate for joy. Or the kind of raw, disarming candour that doesn't ask for approval. She didn't understand what it meant to write something embarrassing and still stand tall next to it.

Sanch was an expert in studying the art of exposure. But she never learned the courage it takes to survive being known.

In the end, that was the difference between us. She borrowed my script but forgot to finish the act.

I did. And I walked offstage with a larger heart, not a bitter one.

CHAPTER 9

One devastating side effect of the access social media gave us—to words, labels and social justice language—is that this very access was born from the fast-moving gears of late-stage capitalism. Our thirst for better, truer words was met with shinier, faster ways to express the mundane violence the gender binary has inflicted on us. We learned how to name abuse with frightening clarity. We began diagnosing everyday power structures with precision.

We weren't wrong, we were ahead of the curve. We knew mental illness was real, yes, but we also knew the diagnosis of borderline personality disorder (BPD) was disproportionately handed to women, while cis-het men were more often labelled with complex post-traumatic stress disorder (PTSD). We understood that psychiatry, like the state and patriarchy, has a long and sinister history of pathologizing human existence, especially the lives of the marginalized.

We learned words like 'decolonization', 'Brahminical patriarchy', 'white feminism', 'savarna feminism'. We navigated our worlds with these terms, wielding them like beautiful weapons against a basic-bitch world. And even though their ideological ancestors had existed for decades, echoed by revolutionaries in every generation, Instagram gave us the illusion that centuries of pain and layered resistance could live neatly inside ten-slide carousels. A punchy caption. The right hashtags.

And there it was: the woke show. A performance I've been a part of, too. Because capitalism and Instagram-far left discourse often resemble the ouroboros, that old image of a snake eating its own tail, trapped in the illusion of renewal. Good intent exists. Some of us use our words wisely. But many are just cannibalizing themselves. And until it's our turn to self-destruct, we play spectators, cheering each other on as we gnaw through our own tendons and bones in the name of being right, looking right, doing right, even if only on our profiles.

At least online, we get to feel in control. Even if it's just for the few seconds of relief that come with a like or a thoughtful comment. Even if it's borrowed righteousness.

So, let's talk about the labels we throw around when we've been hurt: narcissist, sociopath, psychopath.

The truth is, in a grim, postmodern sort of way, the traits we associate with sociopaths—detachment, manipulation, compulsive lying—are typically only diagnosed *after* someone's committed an atrocity. As Patric Gagne,[1] author of *Sociopath: A Memoir*, points out, antisocial personality disorder (ASPD, the more 'polite' term for psychopathy) isn't usually handed out in therapy or clinical evals. It's stamped on court documents. Post-crime. Murderers, stalkers, high-functioning scammers.

Which means our data on sociopathy is contaminated, ruthlessly filtered through punishment, not curiosity.

Gagne herself recalls stabbing a classmate with a pencil as a child, not out of sadism but because it brought her a moment of *relief.* A reset. A pause in the static. It wasn't moral or immoral. It was mechanical.

Now, the DSM, the holy book of American psychiatry, doesn't even list sociopathy as a diagnosis. It lists ASPD, the clinical label most associated with psychopathy. It's tidy. Sterile. It exists to put people into boxes, to help the system do what it does best: manage threats to order.

And make no mistake: the DSM was born in service of the state. Early versions were developed by the US military to assess soldiers coming back from war not quite right. They came back with shell shock. Combat fatigue. The seeds of what we now call PTSD.[2] From the beginning, psychiatry wasn't just about understanding minds, it was about controlling unmanageable behaviour. Often male. Often violent. Often inconvenient.

It's probably because it affected men that PTSD is one of the most familiar mental health terms to us. Men who were needed. Men who had to be patched up and sent back into the capitalist meat grinder. Patriarchy does the darndest things.

When people call someone a 'psychopath', they often mean someone who didn't cry when their dog died or someone who felt nothing at a funeral. But what if the clinical tools we use are measuring not *morality* but *threat*? What if they're less about healing and more about containment?

Jon Ronson, journalist and obsessive chronicler of psychological outliers, asked exactly this in a TED Talk that hit me like a shot of espresso.[3] After years of studying psychopaths and interviewing some of the worst offenders imaginable, he asked: 'Should we define people by the maddest edges of the boxes we put them into?'

The question lingers, not just about *them* but about *us*.

If you want to tumble down the narcissist rabbit hole, Ramani Durvasula's[4] YouTube archive[5] is your entry point. She breaks down narcissism from a protective, public health lens, offering people tools to name and escape manipulation. She also clears up one big confusion:

All psychopaths are narcissists, she says. But not all narcissists are psychopaths.[6]

And sociopaths? Sociopaths, we're told, are *made*, not born. Products of trauma, neglect and environmental chaos.

Psychopaths, on the other hand, tend to show neurological differences. Their amygdala, the part of the brain that processes fear and empathy, often looks different on a scan. Less reactive. More muted.[7] Like someone unplugged the smoke alarm.

They might lie easily, take risks for fun or even steal something petty, not because they need to but because they feel little consequence. Their fear dial is set to low.

Abigail Marsh, a neuroscientist[8] I admire (and frequently argue with in my head), believes psychopathy sits on the same spectrum as extreme altruism. That's right: the cold-blooded scammer and the kidney donor to a stranger might just be cousins on the same neuro-map. According to her research, it all comes down to how we feel fear and how we perceive another's pain.[9] Some of us are hypersensitive. Some of us are switched off. Most of us? We oscillate between the two extremes.

Marsh even claims humans are the most altruistic species in nature.[10] I mean ... sure. Unless you ask any non-human species still trying to live in the ecosystems we're actively burning down. But she has a point: humans are alloparental, we've evolved to care of offspring that aren't biologically our own. Communities that raise each other's children tend to be more empathetic. More cooperative. More generous.

Which raises the question: if empathy is evolutionary, what do we make of those who don't or can't feel it?

Because the story here, my story with Sanch, isn't just about one woman's deception. It's about the *tools* we use to decode harm. About who gets labelled as dangerous. Who gets diagnosed. And who we quietly unfollow.

I don't know if Sanch fits the clinical profile for ASPD. I'm not a psychiatrist and she's not in prison. But I know she lied easily. Repeatedly. Without remorse. I know she could mirror emotion but struggled to sustain intimacy. I know she weaponized stories with surgical precision.

Maybe she sits somewhere on that spectrum.

Maybe we all do.

Because in a world like this, fractured, overstimulated, addicted to performance, it almost makes sense that some of us would grow sharp knives where others grow nerves. That some of us would get numb, check out, lie to get by.

Honestly? I think we all carry a little empathy fatigue. A built-in restraint. A numbness that helps us keep walking past genocides, mass incarceration, child abuse, rape, climate collapse, extreme poverty.

Are we sociopathic for not reacting more? Are we sociopathic for normalizing a world where joy, safety and dignity are luxuries for a few?

What part of us is Sanch?

And what part of us, if we're lucky, is stronger than her?

CHAPTER 10

Gaslighting doesn't always look like someone telling you you're crazy.

Sometimes it looks like a late-night message that says, 'You're making my illness about you.'

Sometimes it looks like a woman with stage-4 cancer telling her boyfriend not to visit because the hospital food is bad and he doesn't speak the local language.

Sometimes it looks like silence, followed by a sudden burst of medical jargon and a blurred photo of a hospital bed.

Looking back, it's bizarre that Ankur didn't just say, 'Fuck this! I'm coming. I love you. I'm going to take care of you whether you want it or not.'

It's strange that I never connected the vague explanations about Sanch's oddly timed radiation sessions. Sure, radiation can technically be an outpatient procedure, but it's brutal, a cumulative treatment that usually leaves people in chronic pain. Sanch never talked about that. She dipped in for radiation as if it were a spa appointment, then breezed out to chat about her life in Delhi. That random Delhi detour—

when Silchar had always been the backdrop—was one of those small, offbeat moments that, in hindsight, cracked open the scale of the con.

But that's the thing when you're in the middle of something that's off, whether it's a con, a toxic friendship or an emotionally abusive relationship. The weight of it accumulates in fragments. You know something is wrong but the wrongness is scattered, slippery enough to evade confrontation. And while you might think it's the small red flags that should push you to act, it rarely works that way. It usually takes something undeniable, like a forged document, a blatant lie, a slap of proof, to finally give you the courage and clarity to call it what it is. Until then, you collect the quiet discomforts and keep moving, hoping you're just being paranoid.

Ankur finally went to Delhi. It was September 2023. Sanch had relented and said he could come for two days. She told him her PG didn't allow men, so he booked a hotel. She promised she'd visit him there.

On the first day, she stopped by for a few minutes, made an excuse and left. Said she was sick. Said she'd meet him after a hospital visit the next day. When she returned the next day, she stayed the night.

But something was wrong.

She was cold. Withdrawn. At times, a complete stranger. She gave glimmers of the 'old Sanch' but they came sandwiched between long spells of silence, distraction, distance. She'd do her own thing. She watched *Modern Family* on Hotstar while sitting next to him, barely acknowledging his presence. Finally, he asked: 'Why are you watching something when we finally have time together?'

She flipped. Like a switch. The warm Sanch returned. She babied him, stroked his hair, gave intimacy. A patch of softness to keep the hope alive. It worked.

And he held on. Because when you've built your reality around someone's story, the smallest sign of tenderness feels like proof that it wasn't all a lie.

The next day, they went to meet a common friend they had got to know online. There, Sanch rattled off crisp, specific details about her college and treatment, information Ankur had never heard before. It wasn't just the clarity that stunned him. It was the confidence. Like she'd memorized a script. He'd only tell me this much later.

They had one more day together. The morning he left, she told him she had to buy ice cream for her roommate. He met her outside his hotel to say goodbye.

The goodbye hug was hollow. Her body felt absent. She didn't kiss him, didn't cry, didn't look like someone parting from a man who had flown different cities to be with her. As he got into the auto, she was already in the shop next door, buying ice cream. She didn't wave. Didn't look back.

By the time he reached Hyderabad, he felt unrecognizable to himself. Empty. Disoriented. Like the trip had rewritten his emotional code. 'I feel like I'm going crazy,' he said to me over a text.

Later, when he was back in Hyderabad, he asked her about the details she had told their friend.

'Bebeee, I already told you these things. You just don't remember,' she said.

Gaslighting in its purest form. Doubt served with a pout.

Ankur knew something wasn't adding up. So did I. But we still couldn't bring ourselves to name it.

At the time, I assumed Sanch was just emotionally overwhelmed. Maybe she was distancing herself from Ankur. Maybe she was shutting down from the weight of her diagnosis. I didn't believe the cancer was fake. That felt too cruel even to imagine. Instead, I gave her the benefit of the doubt. To every doubt she had created. Even when she snapped at me for asking about her health.

'You don't know what it's like to have only a couple of years left,' she said. 'Every time you ask, it reminds me I'm dying. I don't want to talk about it.'

And I froze. Because what do you say to that?

That's the genius of someone like Sanch. She didn't just lie. She built a world where truth felt like a betrayal.

Before gaslighting became a hashtag or the subject of a TikTok, *Gas Light* was a 1938 stage play by Patrick Hamilton, later adapted into a Hollywood film in the 1940s. In it, a man named Gregory marries a woman he suspects is sitting on a hidden fortune. He starts manipulating her reality, flirting with the maids, moving objects and, most famously, dimming the gas lights at night while insisting nothing has changed when his wife notices the flickering. She knows something's wrong. But every time she mentions it, he tells her she's imagining things. His goal? To get her institutionalized so he can claim her inheritance.

The term 'gaslighting' comes from this. It is not just lying but systematically dismantling another person's grasp on reality until they question their every thought, every memory, every feeling.

The modern usage of 'gaslighting' exploded in the realm of psychology and pop culture but here's something wild: it's not even a rigorously peer-reviewed phenomenon in clinical terms. There are no ethical ways to set up experimental groups to gaslight people, obviously. So, what we have instead are patterns. Survivor testimonies. Behavioural case studies. And the bone-deep recognition of what it feels like when your truth is made to seem like fiction.

This is what I have understood about gaslighters. Some do it for power. Others do it, ironically, to regulate their own emotions; by controlling someone else's narrative, they stabilize their own chaos. They undermine their target's ability to perceive and interpret events, not just to deceive but to dominate. The goal isn't just to win an argument. The goal is to crush your version of the world and replace it with theirs.

Which might explain why gaslighting doesn't always show up as aggression. Sometimes it feels like fear. Not yours, *theirs*. A desperate attempt to squash any contradiction to their version of events because they can't afford to feel unstable themselves.

It builds a certain tension in the air. An invisible charge.

You pick up on it, even if nothing makes sense.

Even when the lies are *glaringly obvious*, you hesitate to confront them.

Because somehow, *you* start to feel like the problem.

That's what happened with Ankur. That's what happened with me. We didn't just doubt her, we began to doubt our capacity *to doubt* her.

I met my friend Shalini Rao at a Writing for Resistance workshop I was conducting in 2020 in Bangalore. We became close friends because we have a lot in common. We were aghast at the normalization of low-key, or soft, patriarchy and the abject standards of mental health access in India. Both of us had spent time in San Francisco and Oakland while studying for our master's degrees. Except Shalini was a Gestalt feminist therapist[1] and I was a writer with a master of fine arts (MFA) and in social work.

We started out as protest friends during India's anti-Citizenship Amendment Act protests in late 2019 and early 2020, which for a brief period renewed hope in our democracy. Dozens of cities and towns came together to protest an unfair citizenship act. There was energy. There was art. There was a feeling that maybe things could shift.

Shalini was critical of caste-obsessed India. She had been with her long-term partner Prashant, a playwright and actor. She was queer, sensitive and sometimes made me lose my mind when she asked me to name my feelings about *everything*. I was the tender bully in her life. She was the tender queer therapist who accepted my general inappropriateness and proclivity for saying bluntly awkward things in the middle of an otherwise normal conversation.

Shalini was the first person in my life to show me that my feelings were important. But I was bored by them. Massively irritated, even. Most of my childhood and early twenties had been spent making my way through life with blunt force. I masked, I hid, I wore different personalities depending on who was in front of me. I could feel all the feelings of others but I had no time for mine. They felt like a luxury. An indulgence.

It was always easier to make a reel about something I was righteously enraged about. Or disappear into another mediocre Netflix series. Or welcome being trauma-dumped on, so I could navigate someone else's chaos and avoid my own.

Classic codependency but make it Google-Docs aesthetic. Responding to emotional collapse in bullet points, drafting boundaries in a shared doc titled 'Emotional_Labor-FINAL-V3 (Use This One)' and scheduling my inevitable breakdown via Google Calendar. My inner child had a Trello board. My nervous system was managed via Notion. My grief got stuck in the drafts folder.

At no point did I have a therapist.

And this is exactly where Shalini came in.

She didn't believe in scheduling feelings for later. She would pause mid-conversation to ask what sensation I had in my body. She once asked how I felt while I was trying to order fries. I wanted to throw the menu at her but also ... I weirdly appreciated it.

Because Shalini didn't just ask about feelings. She waited for them. Every conversation had a moment where her face shifted slightly, like she was preparing to receive a fragile package marked 'Handle with care'. No rush. Just the quiet expectation that eventually, I would crack open and say something real.

She made space for discomfort, for naming, for slowness. All the things I bulldozed through because the internet had trained me to respond to life with a clever caption and a crisis post.

I was running from myself. How could I have boundaries or clarity about who I was without doing, well, at least 50 per cent of the work? Of understanding and actually *feeling* my feelings?

She grated on me. But she was right. She was the grounded counterpoint to my chaos.

Today, I look back and see that some of what Shalini said, although it still grates on me, makes sense. She once told me, 'You're just going to do and do and do and then you'll land up in the hospital, completely burned out.' We laughed because it was true and we both have a blunt sense of humour.

My well-intentioned toxic trait is that I compulsively try to connect high-functioning, traumatized people. In my more grandiose visions of my role in life, and to be fair, it does come from a place of genuine generosity, I believe that connecting 'good people' with other 'good people' helps amplify visions, collaborations and, at the very least, our collective imagination.

So, on Sanch's second visit to my house in June 2023, I made sure she met Shalini. More as a mentor than a friend. Sanch had said she wanted to redo her entire undergrad degree to build a foundation in psychology. Shalini held all the depth and range Sanch claimed to admire.

We met at Third Wave Coffee. I opened with one of my characteristically inappropriate intros: 'So this is Shalini, therapist and revolutionary feminist of sorts. And this is Sanch, she's an orphan. But the thing we all have in common is that our dads are dead.'

Shalini chuckled and told Sanch to ignore me. Sanch laughed and said she was used to it.

Within minutes, they were swapping dead-dad stories. Shalini, ever the pro, slowly steered the conversation beyond my jokes and into more meaningful curiosity. She asked Sanch about her goals, her interests, what drew her to therapy. Sanch responded with clarity, listened attentively and took it all in. It was a warm, pleasant hour. Coffee. Banter. Potential.

What I hadn't realized then is that grifters like Sanch love collecting legitimate people. They are always waiting for the next credible connection, the next person they can name-drop, message later for help or their opinions or cite as evidence of proximity to depth. The more such people you're seen around, the easier it is to convince others that you must be good too. Credibility by osmosis.

Sanch hadn't been diagnosed with cancer yet.

But I had already passed on a different kind of malignancy. One that travels quietly through networks of trust.

August/September 2023

By this point, Sanch had found her way into the inboxes of many of my friends and strangers. Her cancer was front and centre, especially after the fundraiser. She spoke to people living with cancer, exchanged notes and built bonds. One story stands out, one I didn't hear until a year and a half later, in early 2025.

Arushi, a beautiful storyteller and founder of the Instagram account Children's Books for All (CBA), had messaged me for a collaboration in 2025. That's when she told me she had connected with Sanch in 2023. Arushi was taking care of her mother who has late-stage cancer. She said Sanch had offered her immense solace, empathy and insight. In return, Arushi gave her support and admiration. She told me she had been in awe of how 'well' Sanch was handling her illness. Today, when we talk about her betrayal, Arushi comes alive with anger. Her mother is still hanging by a thread to her illness and as Arushi prepares for her death, she feels enraged that she had chatted with Sanch, sharing her most vulnerable confessions of fear, grief and the extreme fatigue of being a caretaker to a person who was, for all practical purposes, a ghost of a human being. An illusion of safety and resonance.

That's just one story. I'm sure there are many more. Vulnerable people, those who were suffering from life-threatening diseases or caring for dying loved ones, were brought into Sanch's orbit. I cannot begin to imagine the betrayal they must have felt when they learned it had all been a lie.

It's hard enough for the average person to be vulnerable in this world. When someone like Sanch comes along, it scares people away from ever bonding or opening their hearts again. And that's what enrages me the most. Trust is the foundation of our humanity. It's the force that cracks us open, even temporarily, into something suspended and sacred. When we offer solace to someone in emotional pain, we are participating in the thick, messy, stunning beauty of being human. We were evolved for this, to help, to cocreate, to survive together.

If we let a Sanch ruin that, we risk abandoning the very thing that makes life liveable.

There will always be more Sanchs. Some worse, more dangerous. Some more immature, more parasitic in their relationships. My one book on Sanch won't fix a world that's full of them. As one truth is written, another betrayal begins. That's just the nature of it. But what we *can* hold on to is acceptance, the belief that trying to be decent, wanting to share and collaborate and imagine a world where we can exist and thrive, regardless of gender, class, caste, disability or mental illness is still a fight worth having.

And the only fight you really need to have is with yourself. To keep the most tender, fierce, absurd parts of your humanity alive, to *vindicate* yourself from the fear that one person can take it all away. Because it doesn't end there.

One person scams you. A boyfriend your parents already hated proves them right. A friend you defended turns out to be toxic. The ripple effects are real. People will rush to blame your *humanity* with their favourite weapon: 'I told you so.'

But that 'I told you so'? That's actually the most important part of the story.

If you've been hurt in a similar way, or even if your circumstances are wildly different, I want you to rise above the told-you-sos. Our culture is primed to punish us even when we've been hurt. We're told we should have been more careful, more rational, more circumspect. But that's not how human emotions work.

Most of the fear stitched into our bones comes from authority: our parents, our schools, our institutions, our doctors, our companies. We've never truly been allowed to be fully human in our darkness and flaws. That's the design.

Be too real? That's too scary for most people to deal with. We've been gaslit by entire systems. So, is it really such a stretch to imagine that a person, with reckless energy, no empathy and a taste for high-risk manipulation, could turn that same gaslighting back on us?

The real question isn't how to avoid such people. It's how much of ourselves we're willing to excavate, to find our darkness and our goodness and turn them into *boundaries*. And once we do that, how do we summon the courage to practise them?

Because if there's one thing I know, it's this:

Courage and boundaries are the ingredients that unconditional love is made of.

CHAPTER 11

25 August 2023

On the surface, our WhatsApp group looked like care. But reading through it now, every sentence feels like a carefully laid breadcrumb on a path leading to nowhere. In our larger WhatsApp group set up with online friends from Delhi, Hyderabad and Bangalore, Sanch would steer conversations into seemingly unrelated medical concerns. This group had a couple of people I knew closely and a couple I had never met or interacted with much online.

Sanch: 'Hey Mina, my doctor is suggesting I try Rybelsus. Apparently I'm at high risk for diabetes, both my parents had it in their 30s. He said weight is a factor and I'm kind of chonky. Do you think it's a good idea?'

K: 'It's not diagnosed yet, right? I had pre-diabetes too. My parents are diabetic.'

Sanch: 'I'm almost pre-diabetic and I can't afford to have diabetes with stage-4 cancer. It will fuck me up.'

That phrase 'almost pre-diabetic' nagged at me even then.

It wasn't a diagnosis. It wasn't a real thing.

It was a vague suggestion, wrapped in the urgency of another illness.

But I said nothing.

Not because I didn't notice.

But because noticing would have required confrontation. And confrontation with someone you believe is dying feels like cruelty.

K: 'Exercise, protein, cut sugar—these should help.'

Sanch: 'I can't exercise. I'm too weak from the meds ... Also, I have PCOD [polycystic ovarian disease].'

K: 'Same. Walks help. 30–40 minutes a day. I reversed my pre-diabetes doing that and quitting smoking.'

Sanch: ' 🧚 ' princess kitty sticker

K: 'Pre-diabetes isn't a crisis. I freaked out too.'

Sanch: 'It's the combo that's freaking me out. 😿'

Again, the contradictions stacked up.

Too fatigued to walk but considering a diabetes drug?

And she was going to college?

Said her oncologist suggested Rybelsus but wouldn't name the doctor.

Said it was for diabetes risk—then it became about weight loss.

Still, I said nothing.

I remember thinking, maybe she's just insecure about her weight.

Maybe she wants to lose some for her own reasons.

Maybe this is the one thing she feels she can control.

But something in me, a murky, stubborn part, whispered: She wants to lose weight so it looks like the cancer is doing its job.

A shortcut to a symptom.

I pushed it away.

Because if I believed that ... what else would I have to admit?

Mina: 'Which doctor recommended this? Your oncologist?'

Sanch: 'Yes. It was just a suggestion.'

Mina: 'You should see an endocrinologist.'

Sanch: 'Okay! I'll go tomorrow. I have one. I used to see her for PCOD.'

The next day, the conversation resumed:

Mina: 'Did you go?'

Sanch: 'Yes. She said Rybelsus is doable—not for diabetes but for weight loss. No risks though. She didn't give me a prescription. Said it could help with PCOD.'

Mina: 'But isn't chemo going to cause weight loss anyway? Is this even relevant right now?'

Sanch: 'I mean ... I'm not obese or anything. My BMI is 26.'

That was it. No one responded. We'd run out of responses.

Even I didn't send anything. Not a single message. Because by then, the conversation didn't make sense. It was a spiral, a fog of vague claims and sudden shifts.

Somewhere, beneath my silence, the truth had already landed.

That was August 2023. The last real conversation in the group.

On our personal WhatsApp chats and the Ankur-Sanch-Rheea group, things were tense.

We barely asked her questions, sent the occasional 'Hi, I love you!' message that rarely got a response.

In late December 2023 we got a message from Sanch saying she was going to Silchar for a surgery. We didn't press for details. We knew better.

~

On the night of 5 January 2024, an Instagram account with the username Fairy Lights messaged me. It was Urmila.

> Rheea, Sanch is getting a serious surgery in Silchar but I can only get updates from her cousin sister. I'm in Delhi but will rush to Silchar if things are bad. I'll let you know. Also, I need to ask you—do you think you can get Ankur to break up with her? I don't think she's good for him.
>
> Also listen, whatever you do, both of you don't come to Silchar till I figure out what her health status is and what family is around her. Her entire family is super toxic.

I was stunned. By the message. By the gravity of Sanch's supposed health problems. By the audacity of Urmila's request—for me to ask Ankur to break up with her. And the paranoia about us coming to Silchar uninvited.

It felt more like a performance than a crisis.

I don't remember exactly what I responded, mostly because the account disappeared from Instagram just a couple of days later.

Then, late that night, around 1 a.m., Fairy Lights messaged again.

This time, it sent a message to both Ankur and me: 'I am so sorry. Sanch is no longer with us.'

I was asleep so I didn't see it. But Ankur called me at 1.35 a.m.

When I picked up, he was crying, no, wailing. I had never heard sounds like that from him before. I knew.

He hiccupped and said, 'Did you get the message? She's dead.'

I checked my phone and saw the DM from Fairy Lights.

'Nooooo,' I cried into the phone.

I cried violently, unabashedly.

Utsav woke up, held me, patted my back as I shook on the call with Ankur.

We howled like animals that had been viciously kicked.

And then, just minutes later, a call lit up our WhatsApp group. My heart stopped.

It was from Sanch.

Ankur and I were suspended in disbelief.

A liminal, surreal moment between two realities. After a few frozen seconds, I picked up. Ankur joined in too.

'Sanch? Sanch?'

'Urmila told us you died!'

Sanch's voice came through, healthy. Bright, even.

'Guys! I'm fine! OMG, are y'all seriously crying? I was in the hospital, okay? I had organ failure. It's a thing! My stupid cousin sister called Urmila in a panic and told her I died. She's got mental problems.'

I remember reacting with fury.

'Sanch, this can't just happen. You can't let people think you're dead.'

But she doubled down, unfazed.

'Guys! I'm literally getting discharged from the ICU. My extended family is crazy. It's not my fault! But I'm fine. Please. I'll explain everything tomorrow. Go back to sleep.'

We hung up. Ankur and I were too shocked to call each other again that night. I don't know what he thought about in the hours that followed. I tossed between rage and deep grief, like I was splitting into two selves.

The next morning, I gathered the courage to be as confrontational as I could manage.

I messaged Sanch privately on WhatsApp.

'Sanch, if you don't want us in your life or are having some major spiritual breakthrough while being this ill, just tell us and be clear about it. Being halfway like this is devastating. I won't ask you anything but this is not okay for anyone or anything. It's important to me.'

I was aware my lines weren't coherent. I was trying to muster the courage to confront, to be angry, to be confused. I wasn't sure what I was aiming for; I just knew something was off and, for the first time, I felt like I had the right to question her.

Sanch replied: 'Halfway like what? Please tell me. I was in the ICU yesterday, yet when I woke up, instead of resting, I had to handle a mess I didn't even make.'

I texted: 'That's exactly what I don't understand. Why did it have to be like that? Why won't you trust me with another number from your family? Why do we have to talk to people through a secret account? Why don't we have a working number to get an update? It's not okay what happened last night. You don't owe anyone anything but you must be honest if you don't feel or want to be attached to us like you once were.

'There's no need for BS [bullshit]. I get that you're in a totally different world and looking at life in a way we can't fathom but it doesn't make me less human or vulnerable to the reality of it. Ankur has driven himself mad with helplessness. Just tell him if you want to break up with him. No one is asking you to protect his feelings. This is doing way more harm. And for fuck's sake, if you had doubts about Ankur why didn't you just call me?'

Sanch replied: 'I hear you but it's literally not about trust. I don't have anyone back home who can really relay any information. Urmila is coming today. Harshvardhan isn't picking up my calls. Urmila's number's not working. She's already in the WhatsApp group with you guys.

'Sorry, I meant Harshvardhan is out of the country.'

The incoherence in her messages made me nauseous. They were unaccounted for, like a plastic bottle tossed on a highway.

I responded, 'Urmila doesn't respond most of the time. Tell me, Sanch, you know that wasn't right. Urmila texted me from that fake Instagram account just hours before she said you died and asked me to tell Ankur to break up with you? You were in the hospital then. Why was that her priority? And then your cousin sister supposedly has a breakdown and tells Urmila you died? Ankur and I grieved for you. For whole minutes, we thought you were gone. We were howling.'

'So how am I responsible for this? I was literally in the ICU!'

'I'm just asking you for some goddamn honesty.'

'Rheea, if I didn't want any relationship with you or Ankur, I wouldn't have called you guys right after surgery. I don't know how else to prove I want you in my life or why I should have to prove anything when I am literally dying.'

'Because you are so far away. I know you're the one who's sick but think about it from our side. I know people have let you down but don't push us away just because it's scary. And Ankur… I know there's stuff going on between you two but for his sake, just tell him things aren't the same. If you can't give to the relationship anymore, be honest. Leaving him hanging like this isn't fair.'

She left a voice note. Her voice was low, depleted.

'Rheea, yesterday I was talking to my friend Nimmy. I told her I don't have to carry the burden of her losing me.

And she said that's because our friendship is low-risk and low-entanglement.'

Her voice climbed higher, more emotional.

'But with you guys, it's high-risk and high-entanglement. I try to reassure you; I try to explain. When I talk to Nimmy, it's casual. She just says, "Okay, all the best, you'll be fine." I don't have to do these long-ass conversations with her, updating her about every little thing. I'm literally in the hospital bed right now.'

Her voice broke into half a sob.

I replied, 'I get it but listen, Sanch, I love both you and Ankur. I can separate those relationships. But high-risk and high-entanglement? That's also just life. Real, messy, human life. Shit gets real.'

I admit it, I was swayed again. My love for Sanch and her pain rose against every alarm bell going off. We talked more over text.

She said: 'About Ankur, I told Urmila he was insisting on coming to see me in Delhi when I was super sick and could barely keep up with anything. I vented and she thinks he forced his way to come see me. She doesn't like him because of that. But I can't make her like him! She hasn't met him. She doesn't know he's a good person.'

I replied: 'Can't you just say love is scary? It's a risk for all of us.'

In retrospect, I want to punch myself for how much Hollywood garbage I was texting in that moment. I was desperate. Vacant. Angry.

Sanch texted: 'Fucking say what, Rheea? That I don't want you guys around? Fine. I don't want you guys around! Happy? But it's not true. It's not true. What am I supposed to do? I'm sick as fuck. Have some compassion. Every time I talk to you or Ankur it feels like your feelings about my cancer are more important than the fact that I'm the one who's sick. I know you guys aren't like that, so why do I feel this way?'

'Can you at least tell me why your cousin sister did what she did? Declared you dead? That was a devastating thing to go through. We were destroyed.'

'You know, Urmila wanted to come to Silchar first to validate that I was actually dead. My cousin sister is crazy. That's why she told everyone I died.'

Sanch had already jumped on the idea that we were coming to her funeral. Again, she sent voice notes instead of texts. Our messages had always been a mix of both.

Her voice was high-pitched. Teary.

Every word I heard felt like a twist and yet my heart still clung to the hope there was some truth in all of it.

I said: 'Just know we love you. We're grieving. Give us the power to walk away if that's what you want. But fuck you too for ignoring our pain.'

Sanch replied: 'Listen, my cousin sister got scared because I was in the ICU and she just started telling people I wasn't here anymore. She's also losing someone, okay? It's nobody's fucking fault!'

Then came something especially Bollywood-esque. In a voice note.

'I know you and Ankur must be thinking—why is it only Urmila and Harsh who come see me? It's because my extended family is super toxic. They're already circling me for my property. Asking about wills. So, I can't have you guys here now. They'll treat you badly. The truth is—I did make a will. You and Ankur are in it. That's why you can't come here right now. Please try to understand.'

I replied: 'It's not about the will!'

I didn't know what to say. Why the fuck would she put us in her will?

I felt an alarm scream in my ears.

Yet, I texted back: 'Okay Sanch, I'm sorry. Talk to us when you can. I love you a lot.'

'I love you too.'

Hours later, caffeinated and fed, I replayed the voice notes. Reread the texts. Reviewed the chaos of the night.

My stomach tightened. I felt dizzy. Like the world was collapsing inwards. And then, I popped out of it.

Clarity. Foreign but comforting.

My body released more than six months of gaslighting.

It's funny how one moment you're still doubting, confused, desperate for answers. And then suddenly, your body lets you witness what it knew all along.

The only thing I was sure of now?

Sanch was a liar. And I was going to prove it.

CHAPTER 12

And that's when I decided: if she could lie, so could I. Not to harm. But to test. I crafted the first lie I had ever told her.

'Hey Sanch,' I texted, 'you know that amazing doctor in Silchar you've been talking about? The one you said was treating you? Turns out a journalist friend of mine knows him. Apparently, he's done some really incredible work.'

I waited. Calm. Neutral. What I wanted from her was simple: a crack. A wobble. Evidence, not for others but for myself.

After I dropped the bait about the doctor in Silchar, the lie about the journalist friend, she finally responded.

'Oh yes, he's awesome. He sees a million people though, so I'm not sure he'd even remember me.'

And there it was.

Exactly the kind of thing I knew she would say. Not a reaction to my lie. Not curiosity. Just a quick deflection, a pre-built excuse, a pre-emptive dodge of a question I hadn't even asked.

It was uncanny how predictably she played it. How she always did. But this time, I was actually aware of it. I didn't push further. I just sat back, staring at my phone.

I looked up. Utsav and I were sitting on the sofa.

'I know now,' I said. 'It was all a lie. I just need to figure out how to prove it.'

So, we started back at the beginning.

We pulled up the first medical report, the one we had sent to donors, to doctors, to friends. The one that had been passed around with grim faces and words like 'poor prognosis' whispered in heavy tones. The report that had made everything real.

I had stared at that PDF for months. I had pored over it. Everyone had. But no one, not me, not the doctors, not the friends or fundraisers, had ever thought to scan the tiny QR code in the top corner.

Then Utsav asked the question that changed everything.

'Hey ... did you ever scan this?'

I hadn't. Why would I? We assumed the QR code led to a digital copy of the same report. A formality.

But Utsav, bless his quietly rational brain, opened his camera, hovered it over the code and tapped.

And just like that, everything collapsed.

The link opened a different report. Still for someone named Sanch. But the age listed was twenty, not twenty-seven. And the last name? An upper-caste Bengali one.

Sanch had once told us this name appeared on her Google Pay because her father had legally changed his surname to navigate caste discrimination. She had a whole story. Of course she did.

But that wasn't the shocking part. The shocking part was what the report said.

It was a dengue test. Positive. That's it.

She had dengue. In June 2023.

The report she had passed around, with altered details, a different age, a changed name and a completely fabricated cancer diagnosis, was a recreation of this dengue report.

She had copied the layout. The fonts. The formatting. But she had forgotten one thing. The QR code.

It had taken us six months to get to this moment.

Six months of believing our friend was dying. Six months of raising money. Of sleepless nights. Of texts asking how she was. Six months of thinking: she might not make it.

We had the proof. We had her original report. We had the lie.

Utsav sat beside me in stunned silence. I picked up my phone and called Aparupa.

The next few hours were a blur. Aparupa and I sprang into action like we'd been rehearsing it for months.

I showed her the QR code report. She looked at it, jaw tight, eyes blazing.

'I knew it,' she said.

She had always known something wasn't right. And now, we had proof.

Aparupa, who had actually survived cancer, had the tenacity, clarity and courage to look at the facts without flinching. She wasn't afraid to stare into the rot.

First, she called the testing centre. Calm, composed. She told them she was trying to remember which test she had done at their clinic, a mammogram biopsy or dengue. She said she'd had tests at multiple places and wanted to confirm.

She gave them the report number. The name.

Sanch had never expected her own information to be used against her. She'd passed it around so freely, embedded in WhatsApp groups and tearful fundraiser posts, thinking no one would ever question it.

The clinic got back to us: only a dengue test was done there. Nothing more.

Step one: confirmed.

Then came the bills, those scraps of evidence Sanch had sent to Ankur to justify money from the fundraiser. Some were supposedly from a cancer hospital in Silchar. The headers looked official. The prescription pads had logos.

We picked up the phone.

Aparupa called as the patient. Asked if her records existed. If the prescription number matched someone named Sanchayaita.

The man on the other end took a few minutes. Came back. 'No one by that name in our records.'

We didn't need the extra proof. But it was like watching the floor fall out under her fiction, room by room.

I called Ankur. He was devastated. Still hanging on to some ghost-thread of delusion, convinced that this could somehow still make sense. That maybe it was a mix-up. Maybe there was some explanation.

I told him gently but firmly, 'Ankur, we have to call her. We all need to be on this call. She deserves one last chance to come clean.'

Then I picked up my phone and texted her. Cold. Straight. Final.

'Sanch ... come on.'

She replied within seconds. Like she had been waiting.

'WHAT? What are you talking about?'

That was all I needed to know. She knew. She knew I was on to her.

I didn't waste time. No pleasantries. No leading questions.

'I'm giving you one chance to come clean.'

Sanch replied: 'I have no idea what you're talking about. Can we talk on the phone?'

I could hear her high-pitched voice even through the text. That anxious, performative lilt she used whenever she was spiralling. Seconds later, the voice notes started dropping.

Her voice was shrill. Confused. Angry. Accusatory.

'What are you saying?' 'What are you doing?' 'Why are you messing with a sick person like this?' 'Can we please just talk?'

I added Ankur to the call. All three of us. On the line.

Ankur was still emotionally wrecked. Too disoriented to land any direct confrontation. He was in limbo, half under her spell, half trying to claw his way out.

I took the lead.

'Sanch,' I said, calmly but firmly, 'just tell us. I know you're lying. And you need to come clean.'

That's when she stopped addressing me altogether.

Her voice turned syrupy. Wounded. Manipulative.

'Ankur! Babeeee. Is this really what you believe about me? Ask anyone, ask Nina or Sina or—' [whatever name she could throw in the air for credibility]. 'Ankur! You were in Delhi. You saw the scars. Tell her. Tell her you saw the scars.'

Ankur's voice was shaking. 'Baby … I don't want to be on this call. I just want to understand what's happening.'

Sanch started to unravel.

Her usual clarity, the calculated, sharp-witted cadence she used to control a room, was gone. In its place was high-pitched mumbling. Incoherent sentences. She swung wildly between outrage and desperation.

'How dare you think I'm lying!' Then, without pause: 'Okay, fine. You both come. You both come to Silchar. RIGHT NOW. Come!'

It was the oldest trick in the book. Reclaim control. Deflect. Flood the space with panic and noise.

But this time, I didn't flinch.

Because finally, finally, I could see the truth for what it was: not complicated. Not tragic. Just deliberate.

On 9 January, I got a text from Sanch at 6.06 a.m.

'I think I'll forgive you in the next life besties. I wanted to go in peace and happiness. I want you to know I am at peace and I am happy. Thank you for loving me and believing me for as long as you did.'

Then, at 6.17 a.m. she texted:

'Sent that message by mistake. I had deleted WhatsApp and it was not backed up. Don't worry about it. I am alright don't worry.'

For the first time, I manically laughed. A full-throated, insane chuckle. The illogical message, the suicide note, the retracting of it. She was grasping at straws, panicked, confused, frightened.

I didn't reply.

Instead, I got up from bed and got to work with Aparupa researching any and all details about Sanch. Shockingly, we found her father online using the name we saw on the dengue report. At least, we were pretty sure it was her father. He was listed on a public record online and we found his Facebook profile.

Orphan Sanch had a living, breathing father.

But before we could get into more details, my Instagram and WhatsApp started blowing up with new messages.

They were all from friends and online friends offering me condolences.

> Rheea! OMG I just read Sanch's profile, I can't imagine what you are going through. I knew how close you were.
> Rheea! Is it true? I can't believe it. I am here for you.
> Rheea, just read, I am devastated we were close too, I don't know what we're going to do …

I quickly tapped Sanch's account and checked her story. There was a series of posts, the first saying that Urmila had taken over Sanch's account. Urmila announced Sanch had passed away that morning. Then there was a picture of Sanch and Urmila together with a caption: 'She was gone too soon but she'll be riling up all the right-wing transphobes up there!' Then there was another story with a link to a memorial.

It was beyond comprehension. Sanch had faked a second death. A public one this time. With a digital grave and everything.

The memorial page was on a platform called EverLoved. It read:

> **Sanch February 22nd, 1996 – January 9th, 2024**
>
> With deep sorrow, we announce the passing of <redacted full name> born February 22nd, 1996 and departed January 9th, 2024, at the age of 27. She is survived by her beloved cats Millie, Percy, Chini, Belly and Oppo. Sanch was a formidable force who positively impacted countless lives. A staunch believer in socialism and anti-casteism till her last breath, she remained committed to anti-speciesism throughout her life. She is deeply missed and cherished by many.

This was followed by a link to a fundraiser for the animal rescue she used to support.

I didn't reply to any of the condolence messages. I knew she was alive and had to do something about it. But I still wasn't sure how.

Then at 2.45 p.m., two messages from Urmila came in:

> The Testator devise and bequeathed to Mr. Ankur and Ms. Rheea Mukherjee in joint and exclusive ownership

> the residential property bearing Flat No: 104 situated in Sanhita Apartments, Naktala, Garia, Kolkata, West Bengal – 700047, indicated at SI 4 (11) as above.
>
> The Testator devise and bequeathed to Ms. Rheea Rodriguez Mukherjee, five (5) boxes made of silver for storing vermillion gathered at the residential property with land admeasuring 7,500 sq.ft (10 kathas) bearing House No 52 situated in 2nd Link Road, Lane number-4, Silchar, Cachar, Assam – 788006 as indicated in SI 4(VII).

Soon after we got these badly written fake inheritance texts, we got a PDF with a signature and a lawyer's name saying the same thing.

I cackled. I choked on my laughter. I snorted through tears. I could have never imagined the extent of desperation a con woman might perform when she begins to realize her time is up.

And in that moment, I knew exactly what I had to do. I only half-understood the repercussions of my need to be transparent and warn people. However difficult it was for me to do, I had to come out publicly and tell everyone she was a liar. And she sure as hell wasn't dead.

CHAPTER 13

Transcript of the Instagram video I posted on 9 January 2024

Hi friends,

It's with a very heavy heart that I have to share something incredibly difficult. A person many of us knew, someone I considered a friend, a collaborator, someone who was deeply embedded in several of our circles, has turned out to be a complete con.

That person is Sanch.

The devastating realization of this scam has unfolded slowly over the last couple of months but most potently in the last few days.

This person misrepresented almost everything:

Their age, their identity, where they were from, what they did.

But most disturbingly, Sanch faked having cancer.

And today, she even faked her *death*.

Let me be clear: she is alive.

We have all the evidence.

Earlier, a fundraiser was created to support her supposed cancer treatment. We are now looking into the legal avenues available for those who donated to that fundraiser, including how people can file complaints.

Right now, though, we're still processing.

This has been heartbreaking. I can barely think straight but I knew I had to tell you this as quickly as possible, because we are all so interconnected here on Instagram.

Thank you for listening. Please hold on for updates. We'll be sharing more as we learn more.

~

April 2024

Three months had passed since I had published my video. It had amassed over 85,000 views in the first few days, which, on the surface, could have looked like a moment of triumph. Inspirational, even. But no one, except maybe a couple of friends, knew the extent of what I was going through. And even they didn't know the half of it. Because I didn't either.

Shock. Chaos. Scandalous rumours. Police reports. Life-threatening depression. It all collided like a slow-motion car crash I couldn't look away from. And yet, I kept showing up.

At the time, I was heading branding for a fintech company. Eleven months in, six of those overlapping with Sanch's 'cancer' timeline, I was stuck in a job that didn't align with my values. Yet, I had built something meaningful: a small but remarkable team. That team ended up being part of what saved me.

One of them was a designer I'd worked with years ago, back when I co-ran a content studio. We'd lost touch for a while, then reconnected in early 2023, both of us burned out in different ways. We fell back into rhythm quickly, both creatively restless, both working at a company that was beginning to gnaw at our insides.

A couple of months in, we needed to hire a videographer. We put out a call on LinkedIn and were met with the usual flood: overconfident men, bland reels, tepid emails. I was seconds away from deleting the entire post when Sahithi's portfolio landed in my inbox. Nothing flashy. No fake polish. Just a short documentary on Pottery Road that had soul. Her camera lingered. Her edits breathed. I sent it to my designer colleague with one line: 'This is her.'

Sahithi had no real interest in fintech. She'd applied to dozens of jobs out of necessity more than desire. She was twenty-four years old. No one knows what they're doing at twenty-four.

She called us 'ma'am' in the interview. We told her to knock that off immediately. We were far more chaotic and irreverent than our titles implied. Later, she told us she only accepted the job because, in her words, 'You both seemed fun.' Which sounds about right.

Two weeks later, she moved to Hyderabad, found a PG and walked into the office on the eve of her birthday. I was technically her manager but, in truth, I was slowly becoming her unofficial mentor-mother-auntie hybrid.

Sahithi had long black hair, a face made for South Indian cinema and a near-manic curiosity about everything. She wasn't a reader. She wasn't into political discourse. Her grammar was terrible. Her sense of style was fresh, not flashy. She loved Indo-Chinese food with the intensity of a teenage romance: glossy noodles, extra Manchurian, deep-fried flour-coated paneer. I hovered like a tragic auntie at a wedding, dishing out unsolicited advice about gut health, processed sauces and the inevitable betrayal of her digestive system.

But the girl could shoot. She could edit. She could tell a story in thirty seconds that made you feel something. Her thirst to capture light, motion and texture, paired with an inimitable instinct for music, made her a natural. And despite the gulf between us—generational, political and intellectual—I trusted her. Deeply. Her heart had integrity. Her kindness was active.

She wasn't like the friends I was used to. She didn't cite bell hooks. She didn't rage about politics or perform her progressive ideology on cue. But she cared. Genuinely. And I was learning to care about more than principles that aligned on the surface level.

My designer colleague and I, on the other hand, were textbook progressives. Performing our moral frustration between Canva decks and Instagram stories. We planned protests for Palestine in the same breath we packaged fintech propaganda as financial empowerment for Instagram. We raged. We overshared. We spiralled.

Sahithi just watched. Quiet. Curious. And we didn't push her. That mattered.

Because if this era has taught me anything, it's that ideological saturation is real. People pick up rhetoric for all kinds of reasons: loneliness, trauma, anxiety, identity, fear. Not everyone arrives at politics through books. Some get there through heartbreak. Some never get there.

Courage doesn't always look like confrontation. Sometimes, it looks like curiosity. Like letting someone grow in their own time.

That's what Sahithi reminded me of. That's what I tried to practise with her.

My designer colleague had rejoined the team right around the time Sanch was 'diagnosed'. Sahithi had come in a couple of months later, in August 2023. By then, Sanch had already been mythologized in our world as the brilliant, tragic friend of mine with stage-4 cancer.

So, while we were building decks and shooting explainer videos, they were also witnessing my emotional wreckage unfold in real time. They heard fragments of doubt, then horror, then cold certainty. They stood by me as the truth detonated in January 2024.

They were there through the messages, the harassment, the panic attacks. They saw it all. And somehow, from that wreckage, something resilient began to take root.

By May 2024, we had walked out of the fintech job and started something of our own: Moonbird Creative. Something alive. Something honest. Something that could only grow out of the kind of grief no one volunteers for.

But before we get there, before the phoenix rises and all that, there's the fallout.

The grief. A peculiar misery one must endure for outing a scammer.

It starts off almost noble. You think: I'll tell the truth. I'll admit I was fooled. I'll warn others so they don't have to feel what I did.

Adorable.

Because here's the thing: the truth doesn't sound brave to people. It sounds accusatory.

It doesn't land like clarity. It lands like insult.

Because when you say, 'I was conned,' people often also hear, 'And so were you.'

And no one likes that reminder. No one wants to be the fool. And certainly not in public. I wasn't just outing a scam. I was lighting a match under everyone's denial.

And for that, I was about to pay.

CHAPTER 14

Moments after I posted the video outing Sanch, I felt like I was coated in a redemptive balm. A strange stillness took over. I had done the right thing and that feeling, peace or something like it, lingered, even as more details surfaced about the extent of the lies with which Sanch had pranced her way into the internet.

But before that calm could settle, my inbox exploded again. At first, it was all messages of shock. A few kind souls even asked how I was doing. But then the bile began to seep in. After all, I couldn't yet prove that Sanch wasn't dead. Her stories announcing her death, and then her entire Instagram page vanished moments after my video went live.

A friend texted me a screenshot.

'Did you see what Sanch messaged someone?' It must have been Urmila who wrote it. Or Sanch herself.

The message had been sent to some stranger online I didn't know:

'Hey, so the truth is some savarna woman didn't believe Sanch had cancer and started questioning her. She was so heartbroken she overdosed on morphine the next morning. She couldn't take her friend's betrayal.'

So now I was the 'savarna woman' who pushed her to suicide?

Incredible. And painful. But still nothing compared to what was about to come: the conspiracy theories, the projection, the pure vitriol I'd be subjected to for weeks.

People put up Instagram stories accusing Ankur and me of being in on the scam.

The theory: something must have gone wrong. There was a fight about the money. I had called her out as revenge.

It was laughable.

But at the time, it felt like being shot on the limbs. Inside, I was crawling, weeping.

More stories started surfacing.

'We've always known Sanch was a scam.'

'She bullied us during the Clubhouse days too.'

'Don't tell me Rheea didn't know.'

Only one intersectional vegan account stayed faithful and fair. She put up stories in solidarity, asking people to shut the hell up with their conspiracy theories.

'If you all *knew* this entire time,' she asked, 'why didn't you say anything?'

Some newspapers reached out for the story. I kept it factual. I told them about the QR code and what it had revealed. I gave them the timeline. I answered the questions I could manage.

Meanwhile, Aparupa had found more damning revelations. With Sanch's full name confirmed and her father's name too, Google began serving up pictures of her from high school.

Sanch wasn't twenty-six.

She was nineteen, maybe twenty, when she had scammed all of us into believing she was older.

One photo hit me like a brick. She was in a maroon blazer and school skirt which stopped just below the knee. Thick glasses. Short hair ending at the lobes. A group of students grinning around her, hoisting a quiz trophy. She looked geeky, wide-eyed, utterly different from the cool, city-girl persona she had used online.

I felt bile rise in my throat.

She had grifted me, I who am middle-aged, allegedly wise, with a clarity and skill that was terrifying.

Ankur had a harder time. Not only was the internet accusing him of being part of the scam but now he had to process the fact that he had been dating someone far younger than she had claimed to be. She even had a fake Aadhaar card listing her age as twenty-seven.

That first night, I played along. People had questions. The DMs kept coming. Utsav came to me and said, 'I'll take half. I'll start replying.'

So, I began directing people to him. 'Message my husband,' I typed, over and over.

'He'll help answer anything I can't right now.'

He sat in the little office room, hunched over his phone, responding with clarity and kindness to the well-meaning ones.

I sat outside, trying not to fall apart.

The next morning, Aparupa came over. We had Sanch's father's phone number and we were going to call him. I put him on speakerphone so Aparupa could be there to offer me moral support.

He picked up. He sounded like any older uncle—gentle, a thick Bengali accent, a little confused.

Aparupa said, 'Uncle, we're trying to locate Sanch. She's our friend and we can't trace her.'

He replied, 'She was here just a little while ago. But she's out now. Should I tell her to call you back?'

'Yes but could you please reconfirm her number?'

He gave us the same number we already had. I hadn't checked if it was still active. Ever since her bizarre suicide message, which she retracted minutes later, I hadn't known what to believe.

Aparupa was quiet for a second before asking gently, 'Uncle, there's something we need to tell you. Are you Sanch's father?'

'Yes, of course,' he said casually, like it was the most obvious thing in the world.

I cleared my throat. 'Because she told us you died in 2021 from cancer.'

Silence. Thick. Static. The kind you feel more than hear.

'What?' he said, after a pause.

'And,' I added slowly, 'she told us her mother passed away when she was sixteen.'

'She's very much alive,' he replied. 'She's in the next room.'

Aparupa took the lead again, her voice steady but soft with a quiet anxiety. 'Uncle, this is really difficult for us to say and we're trying to handle this in a way that's fair to everyone but we need your help. Did you know Sanch has been telling people she has stage-4 cancer? For the past six months?'

She looked over at me.

'She faked her death online yesterday,' I added.

There was a strange sound on the other end, an awkward chuckle.

'No, no,' he said. 'She was telling me something about this. Some group of bad friends were using AI to manipulate her social media. It's all fake news. They're using AI tools.'

I nearly lost it.

'No, Uncle,' I said. 'This is not AI. I met her. We did a fundraiser. The public gave over four lakhs for her cancer treatment. I have videos.'

'This is serious,' Aparupa said. 'We have to act.'

I scrambled to find an old video, one of Sanch talking about her illness and sent it to him on WhatsApp. Her face. Her voice. Her lie.

'Please just watch the video,' I said. 'It's not AI.'

His tone changed immediately. Something dropped. He had seen her. Heard her. The denial didn't stand a chance.

'I don't know what to say,' he murmured. 'Maybe she's fallen into very bad company. How much money did she take?'

'Around four and a half lakhs,' Aparupa replied. 'But we don't know if that's everything. She's taken money for other things—flood relief, animal rescue. We don't know if any of it ever reached where it was supposed to.'

'She has a criminal mindset,' he said. Slowly. Softly. Like a man realizing he didn't know his own daughter.

'Together, we can figure this out,' I told him. 'But she owes the public an apology. And you need to talk to her first.'

'I'll confront her when she gets back,' he said. 'I'll update you.'

'Thank you, Uncle,' we said together. 'You've been genuinely helpful during a very distressing time. We hope to hear from you soon.'

We cut the call. We sat there, stunned. We couldn't believe what we'd heard. But instinctively, we also knew: a father will protect his daughter. He may have been caught off-guard and submitted to honesty but would it last? Would Sanch manipulate him too?

Meanwhile, the internet had lost its mind again. Twitter caught wind of the scandal. Someone created an entire thread speculating on what happened, using fragments from my video, mixed with broken facts and wild conspiracies. According to one version, Ankur and I were the masterminds behind the scam who'd had a falling out with Sanch and so I had decided to go public for revenge.

I felt panic. I felt stupid. Most of all, I felt hurt.

People I had followed for years, people who commented on my posts, people I had helped, whose work I had edited, for whom I'd written recommendations, offered support to were suddenly silent. Or worse, joining the conspiracy dogpile.

Within forty-eight hours, two anonymous Instagram accounts popped up. One of them had a glorified photoshopped picture of Sanch smoking a cigar as the profile image. The handle was called @SanchScam and the bio claimed it was an 'unsolicited public service to uncover the real story'.

This account started targeting Ankur. Sanch had done some triangulating before her grand exit, planting enough dysfunction and toxicity across multiple circles that a few people, especially from her time in Hyderabad, latched on to the lies. I won't get into all of it. I've promised dignity to the ones who were hurt and unfairly villainized during this fallout.

And yes, that includes people who were, and still are, known grifters in the anti-caste space. But here's what I've learned the hard way:

People who've decided to project their hate and insecurity on to you will do it no matter what. Even your silence will provoke them. And if it does?

I can tell you now—I don't give a flying fuck anymore.

It is true, however, that I harmed a person I knew by choosing to believe Sanch over them.

I've apologized. They've wished me well. But they don't want me in their life anymore.

I respect that.

For a while, I flipped into cool, black-humour Rheea. I posted jokes about being duped by a girl half my age. I answered questions on Instagram stories. I performed my breakdown.

When the aftermath of Sanch's lie was at its most potent, my friend Vani Subramanian, who'd got her friends to donate to the fundraiser and even sent a care package to Sanch, had told me to slow down, to not feel the need to overextend myself to strangers on the internet. 'You don't owe everyone an explanation,' she said. 'You did your job. You outed her. Now you're just feeding the vultures.'

Now, I had put her in a position that had her shamefully apologizing to the friends she had outside India who had generously donated to Sanch.

But there was more to it than just apologies. The betrayal from progressive circles, the cruel silence from people I'd helped, it all broke me.

Then there were the donors. Furious, obsessed with refunds. No questions about how I was. No curiosity about what we could do together to fix it.

Sanch had burned my entire fundraising credibility to the ground.

She had DMed people asking for money too. This didn't start with cancer. It started long before, with flood-relief scams and animal-rescue grifts. I can only say this with the clarity of my experience but I can't prove it because those funds never hit our circles—we only gave to them.

~

And then, Aparupa tried her number.

Sanch picked up.

Aparupa asked directly: 'Hi Sanch, do you have cancer?'

Sanch replied, her tone casual, unfazed, 'No. I had dengue.'

She hung up.

The number never worked again.

I knew what I had to do: file a report.

But Ankur backed out. He was terrified. His family was terrified. The police might implicate him.

'You gave her the money,' I said.

'Yes,' he said. 'And I have all the receipts. I've sent them to you. But I can't do this. My family won't let me.'

I was angry. But I also understood. He was a Dalit man, trying to survive, already under suspicion.

We agreed to stop talking. It wasn't healthy. I missed him every day. For a year, he disappeared.

I wouldn't hear from him again until Sana told me to reach out to him for this book.

I had never filed a first information report (FIR) in my life. Utsav and Aparupa came with me.

We sat on metal chairs, waiting. A policeman called us in.

Utsav and Aparupa explained the issue in Kannada. The officer listened.

'Hundreds of fraud cases every day, madam. Most are in crores. But write your complaint. We'll see,' the policeman said.

He handed me a pen and a piece of white paper.

'Address it to the head inspector. "Dear Sir ..."'

It felt like something out of a British colonial drama. I sat. I wrote.

'Dear Sir.'

I hiccupped. Then sobbed.

Aparupa and Utsav took turns patting my back.

Tears splashed on to the paper. I wiped them and kept writing.

I couldn't include the emotional devastation, the shame, the panic. But I did what I could.

One of the officers looked at me, half amused, half compassionate.

I took a breath and began again.

This was the beginning of the end.

Or maybe, the end of the beginning.

CHAPTER 15

In the last few years, the FedEx scam and its garden-variety copycats[1] have brought a fresh wave of panic to WhatsApp groups and local media. These scams are emotionless and mechanical, engineered for speed and to generate confusion, built to exploit one-time passwords (OTPs) and anyone slightly more trusting than they should be. This includes baby boomers, Gen X-ers and, yes, let's not forget us geriatric millennials. I believe we're more likely to defer to anyone on the phone who sounds confident, spews banking jargon and uses customer-service-speak like it's a sacred dialect.

For the uninitiated, the FedEx scam starts with a simple message: a package from a foreign country is stuck and you must press 1 to speak to an agent. That's it. Your curiosity is baited. Your ego is involved. 'Did someone send me something? An old friend? A distant relative? What's in that damn package?'

You press the button.

The 'agent' answers kindly. Someone from Australia, Dubai—or even Iran—has sent a package. The contents? Some random items and a quarter kilo of narcotics.

Your heart skips.

'There must be some mistake,' you offer. 'I don't know anyone there.'

The agent calmly confirms your phone number, your address, sometimes even your Aadhaar. Now you're really sweating.

They tell you that customs is involved. A fake police officer comes on the line, stern and unwavering: either get to Mumbai immediately or prepare to be arrested at home. You're caught in psychological warfare.

People have reportedly lost lakhs paying off these 'officials' to sweep their fictitious drug problem under the carpet. But it escalates. Ask for a lawyer and the voice on the other end turns colder.

'I don't think you understand the Narcotics Act, sir. You'll be taken into judicial custody until you get a lawyer.'

Some victims report being manipulated into a kind of digital house arrest—forced to stay glued to their screens, phones off, while being mentally cornered into compliance.

These scams work because they exploit people's fears, their respect for authority and their sense of shame. Today, most folks hang up the moment the caller says 'FedEx', but this game still claims new victims every day.

Me? I sniff these scams a mile away. Sometimes, I indulge these scam callers, stringing them along until I get bored and say something like, 'Okay, I'm done now but does this job really nourish your soul?'

Once, I did this to a FedEx scammer. He didn't curse. He laughed.

'Ma'am,' he said, 'truth is, it does. I get a lot of pleasure from this. It helps my soul. Goodbye. Have a nice day.'

I barely managed a stunned, 'Touché.'

This was a reminder: manipulation and gaslighting wear many faces. And some people, astonishingly, get a kick from it.

But the scams we're *emotionally* ill-equipped to deal with? They're not the ones that occur over the phone. They're the ones at home.

Picture this:

You're a middle-class urban Indian kid. You learn early—subconsciously—that the adults around you are inconsistent. Mom gets teary when Dad's stressed because he takes it out on the dinner she made. Your parents have yelled at you for bad grades, disrespecting elders or hiding a teenage relationship. But they've also taken you out for Sunday dosa. They've made your favourite birthday meals.

Your childhood was full of contradictions.

Your future? Already charted. Science stream. Engineering. Doctor, maybe. Or business, if your parents are slightly more liberal. You're too dependent on them to rebel and too insulated to imagine another path. If your mother isn't the kind to say to your father, 'Screw you, Ramesh, you don't like my food? Cook your own damn dinner,' you likely don't even know it's possible to stand up for yourself.

Eventually, you'll marry. Class and caste aligned. Kids will follow.

And maybe, your spouse will mirror the same systems you grew up with. You ask to go to a movie. They say, 'We just went last Sunday.' You know you didn't. But you drop it. You want peace more than truth.

They cheat. You see the texts. They say, 'We were rehearsing for an office skit.' Ludicrous but you stay quiet.

They empty your joint savings. You protest. They respond, 'So, travel is more important than my business?'

These aren't just personal betrayals. This is what American psychologist and researcher Jennifer Freyd calls 'betrayal trauma'.[2] And to survive it, your body may enter a state she named 'betrayal blindness', a survival mechanism. You may feel numb. You may forget whole incidents. You may feel like the crazy one.

Freyd coined the term 'DARVO' to explain this exact manipulation pattern. DARVO stands for Deny, Attack and Reverse Victim and Offender.

It's a favoured tactic among narcissists, people with ASPD traits and institutions trying to save face. It's emotional abuse with a PR strategy.

And here's where things get horrifyingly meta.

Jennifer Freyd recovered memories of her own childhood abuse—committed, she says, by her father. When she confronted her parents, they denied it. Not only that—they launched a full-fledged attack against her. They wrote to her university, calling her unstable. They even formed the False Memory Syndrome Foundation, attempting to discredit not just her story but her entire field.

Freyd's theory played out in real time:

D: They denied the abuse.

A: They attacked her professional credibility.

RVO: They reversed the roles, casting themselves as the victims of a mentally ill daughter.

If you're reading about DARVO for the first time, take a breath. This tactic isn't reserved for classic villains. It shows up in regular people—those who are emotionally immature, selfish or terrified of accountability.

And when you've grown up trained to preserve peace at all costs? You won't even know it's happening.

We are wired for connection.

Ramani Durvasula, who has spent years deconstructing toxic dynamics, says it plainly: 'We're social animals. We want people. Even the ones who neglect us. Even the ones who twist our minds like wrung-out dish towels. We stay, often not out of ignorance but because we've been trained to live with contradiction. The world is full of them, after all. A country can be secular on paper and oppressive in practice. A parent can tuck you in at night and tear you down by morning. A partner can gift you love on Thursday and gaslight you on Friday.'

We get used to the inconsistency. We call it life.

But the worst part of being gaslit, again and again, is this:

You believe it's your fault.

Because the manipulator tells you so.

'You don't remember it right.'

'You always do this.'

'I think you need to go back to therapy—you're not making sense lately.'

You start to wonder if they're right.

And it's not just emotional manipulation—it's a social threat. If you're a woman, queer, trans, neurodivergent, Dalit, Muslim, broke or any combination of identities that hinder you from walking safely through this world, leaving can mean risking everything. You may stay with a cheating husband not because you're in love but because you have a baby, no money and are part of a culture that will spit you out for daring to want something else.

Some people can't leave for material reasons. And that's real. But many more of us stay because we've never been taught that leaving is even an option.

If you weren't raised around people who showed you what boundaries look like—people who speak calmly, hold firmly and respect you without drama—you might not even recognize what abuse is.

Safety, to you, might have always been a mixed bag: denial, rage, whimpers and 'making the best of it'.

Maybe someone told you: 'At least you have this. Without me, you'd have nothing.'

That isn't love. That's manipulation dressed up as salvation.

So, how do you begin to reclaim yourself?

Durvasula says it starts with meeting yourself exactly where you are. Not in denial. Not in some fantasy future. Right here. In the muck. You may not be able to leave right away. You may not even *want* to leave. But you can start learning to disengage. You can start building small boundaries, one brutal centimetre at a time.[3]

Say someone tells you, 'But I told you we had to be there at 7 p.m. today.'

But you know, you absolutely know, they never said that.

Instead of falling into the trap, you reply:

'Well, we clearly have very different memories of that. I didn't hear that from you.'

Then stop.

Do not chase the thread.

Don't fall into the rabbit hole.

This, Durvasula says, is one of the first survival tools: refusing to descend into the spiral of defending your reality. Because what the manipulator wants is to twist it until you think it's your job to untangle it.

It's not.

When you believe it's your fault, you believe you can fix it. That's the trap.

But this isn't your flaw.

It's their pathology.

And just knowing that, even standing at the edge of that realization, can crack open a little room inside you. Room to breathe. Room to say, 'Maybe it's not me.' Room to say no.

You won't heal in a linear arc. You may not even heal all the way. But you can start to notice what doesn't sit right. You can mark it: That felt unsafe. That felt off. That hurt.

And then, when you're ready, you can walk, not run, towards the kind of love and care that doesn't require you to explain yourself out of your own sanity.

When it came to Ankur and me, we were the perfect ingredients for Sanch's scam soufflé. Ankur brought the thirst for love. I brought the saviour complex. She brought the lies and mixed it in like cake batter. Ankur stayed loyal like it was *Kaun Banega Gaslight Victim*, praying for a lifeline that never came.

I was Kokila Ben, sternly guiding Gopi Bahu aka Sanch toward her inner greatness.

Just turns out I was just another kitchen utensil in her emotional Rasoda.

We were marked in different ways but carried the same ghost. The scam ended in six months. The haunting stayed for much, much longer.

CHAPTER 16

I am ferally fatigued and cosmically underwhelmed by the burden of being a good person.

All my life, I've tried to do the most ethical thing, be the most emotionally present friend, be overly generous with my money, call out immoral bullshit—from nosy aunties scolding a teenager for wearing shorts to once screaming at a gang of boys trying to kidnap stray puppies in broad daylight.

They were shoving them into a bag, planning to kill them 'before they became a nuisance'. I unleashed a banshee-like shriek. Neighbours poured out of their homes. The boys let the puppies go. And for many nights afterwards, I couldn't sleep because I knew they'd just wait for another evening, a darker corner, a moment without witnesses.

If so much bad exists and if my brain's been hardwired for excessive empathy, then being good hasn't been a choice. It's been a hostage situation.

And the funny part? To the outside world, at least when I used to care what the outside world thought, I was never really seen as 'good' in the first place.

I failed in school. Not dramatically but just enough to be shunted out of the sciences into the arts. In the early 2000s, that was its own quiet humiliation. Arts was the stream of the soft, the failed, the futureless. Unless you had elite connections, it meant marriage was your career goal.

Then came the commentary on my body. 'Too pretty to be chonky,' the aunties whispered, as if that was a compliment.

Then came marriage number one. A big fat Indian wedding in Jaipur. The kind of wedding that now makes me nauseous to think about because my values have long since changed. But back then, I followed the script. I played the part. One year later, we were divorced. Another failure.

This woman? Divorced by twenty-two? With only a social work degree in her back pocket?

Neighbourhood aunties and uncles tsked. 'Rheea's lost her mind,' they said. 'She needs to take life seriously.'

And then, because shame loves momentum, I rushed into marriage number two just two and a half years later.

This one looked perfect. He was a kind, hardworking man. We lived in San Francisco. I was doing my MFA. He made good money. We had a shared history in Bangalore. He was even willing to move back to India.

We lasted four months after returning to India. My father died. The grief was mine but society made it his. 'She's not herself.' 'She's broken.' 'It must be the loss of her father.'

No one wanted to see that I simply didn't fit into the role of a wife, at least not the way I was supposed to.

So, I had an affair with an old family friend. My mother called me selfish. People called me unstable. Even my closest friends seemed to back away. I felt their disappointment in waves, like I'd shattered their idealized version of my life in my nice apartment right off dusty Outer Ring Road.

But when we separated, I was fair. In both marriages, I never imagined asking for alimony. The idea disgusted me. I had to take ownership.

And so, at twenty-eight, I stood in a barren apartment—no joint account, no man to fall back on. Just me, the wind and my then rebonded, poker-straight hair.

That's when I decided to hustle: run workshops, take content gigs, build a life brick by brick.

And strangely, that's when I first felt a glimmer of something that resembled pride. I wasn't good, necessarily. Not in the traditional sense. But I was becoming me. And to get there, I had to be selfish. Ruthless, even.

The shame? It stayed. Like a light winter jacket, not heavy enough to suffocate me but always there: itchy, hot, unnecessary.

Even in my so-called 'bad girl era', I was kind. I spoke up. I mentored. I told people not to take advice but to exchange stories, to cross-pollinate their pain and joy and find human truth.

I used to think Machiavellian meant heartless. Cold. Strategic to the point of sociopathy.

However, when you research him, even lightly, you'll find there was a certain rigour in his approach. A praxis he created that could be erased from our minds when we imagine a caricature version of a tyrant. Machiavelli, a political thinker during the Renaissance, didn't believe in morality as a guiding force. He believed in efficiency. And that efficiency earned you power, respect and fear. His world wasn't about kindness. It was about control.

So, I asked myself: What the hell have I been doing for the last fifteen years?

I've practised what I call *radical kindness*, a kind of kindness that's inconvenient. That makes people uncomfortable. It's not offering tea to your auntie. It's pulling a woman out of danger on the street. It's showing up at a protest. It's helping a sick dog. It's cooking every day for an elder in your neighbourhood who has no one else.

These things disrupt polite society. They subvert convenient morality.

But Machiavelli would laugh. Because he knew something I hadn't wanted to admit:

'People don't act motivated by your goodness. They act driven by interest, fear and power.'

Unless your kindness gives you influence, it doesn't make you powerful. People won't seek your friendship for your ethics, they'll do it for your access, your image, your social clout.

'You may be the most just person in the world. But if you seem weak, you will be treated as weak.'

'You may have the most generous heart but if you do not inspire respect, you will be ignored.'

With Sanch, I thought compassion would protect me. I offered support. I ignored my instincts. I explained away red flags.

She played me. Not because I was dumb but because I believed that being good was enough.

'Everyone sees what you appear to be. Few feel what you really are.'

I believed that generosity, integrity and intention would build a life that would reward me in kind.

But Sanch saw that belief and sharpened it into a weapon. She used my kindness against me.

So, I ask: Is kindness still a virtue? Or is it just a delusion? A boundaryless hope that someday, people like her will be the exception and not the rule?

But I haven't told you the thickest part of my pain yet.

I tucked it all the way near the end of this book like a bruise under a sleeve, too embarrassing to show, too festering to ignore.

In 2023, *The Girl Who Kept Falling in Love*, my second novel, was published by Hamish Hamilton, Penguin India. It was released in September. That was the same time Sanch was 'dying of cancer'. We were four months away from the unravelling.

She had already read *The Body Myth*, my debut. I'd sent her a signed copy, of course. She sent back glowing voice notes. Told me she loved it. Complimented how I'd managed to write urban Indian fiction without exoticizing it for a Western gaze. She was sharp like that.

By the time my second book was about to hit the press, Sanch was telling us she had around six months to live.

And I, still soaked in projection, still riding the coattails of her tragedy, dedicated the book to her.

It wasn't her idea. It was mine. The wounded older sister inside me insisted on it. I had thought she was going to be a brilliant writer one day and had believed in her long before she ever got sick. I sent her a message asking if she'd be okay with it.

She wrote back: 'Are you really sure you want to do that for me? Like … really?'

I said yes. And I did.

The book says '*For Sanch*' on its dedication page.

To this day, I can't hold my book without feeling disgust coil inside me. There were so many others who deserved that space. But my obsession, my theatre of grief, made me choose her.

She read it. Eventually. Said it was nice. Said she still preferred *The Body Myth*. I laughed and told her, 'Honestly, so do I.'

Months later, she 'died' on Instagram. Then deactivated her page.

Then the @SanchScam page blew up.

The trolls came for us. Some stranger even sent me a screenshot of a WhatsApp message Sanch had sent another friend I didn't know:

'Hey, I need some advice. A writer friend of mine just sent me her book to read and it's really bad. But the thing is, she dedicated it to me. So I'm not sure what to say back. Got any thoughts?'

What hurt wasn't that she thought the book was bad. Books are subjective. If she'd told me she hated it, I'd have probably cackled with her.

No. The pain was in the betrayal of intimacy. The quiet backchannel manipulation.

Sanch didn't just critique me. She used me—as content, as status, as a character to boost herself. She strategized her interactions with us the way you'd plan a networking event: ask for advice to make someone feel important, name-drop someone to establish power, act cool about it to claim superiority.

All the while, to Ankur and me, she played the role of a devoted friend. The grateful patient. The honest comrade.

But the truth is, her soggy, tepid soul was always analysing opportunities behind our backs. She was strategic when it mattered and virtuous when it was convenient.

She was Machiavellian, through and through. And maybe, if she had been a politician, she would have won.

But even Machiavelli couldn't have predicted Instagram would be her battlefield and betrayal her brand.

CHAPTER 17

I sat cooped up in my house for over two days, rehashing the incident, answering questions, explaining the hows, whats and whens. Ultimately, everyone was asking the same thing under varying shades of concern, anger or judgment: 'What are you going to do about it?'

I went back and forth about filing a police complaint. The social-justice warriors had already sharpened their knives—'Does Rheea believe in carceral punishment?' they asked—while others accused me of having enabled Sanch for too long. The inanities and insecurities of people ballooned into their most voyeuristic urges. Public shaming, of any kind, would do. And in the Petri dish of small, incestuous social media circles, the scandal felt fresh, hot, almost erotic. For a second, everyone was collectively dredging up their own Sanch histories.

Some of her more vocal supporters, people who had promoted her fundraisers long before the one for her cancer treatment, went silent. Bigger influencers chimed in with curated commentary. I had a front-row seat to watch how factual reporting, conspiracy theory, online drama, voyeurism and the gnawing fear of one's own DMs being exposed, all collided to form a collective credibility crisis.

Meanwhile, mainstream media had picked up the story. *The Economic Times* ran a piece on the cancer scam. Other online outlets followed, most of them citing my video. That, at least, was a relief; there were no wild spins or wacky conspiracy angles I had to battle. A few journalists reached out to me and took furious notes.

Ankur had reason to freak out. Months before the cancer arc, Sanch had orchestrated a quiet witch hunt against him. She'd done it to play the 'good girlfriend' online, defending her man publicly, only to use it against him when she 'died'. I don't want to pick at Ankur's wounds nor do I want to rob him of the right to tell his story on his own terms. But I'll say this: the number of 'mini' scams Sanch pulled on us, even during the good times, is incalculable. Sometimes, it's hard to forgive myself for being that trusting.

Still, there were incredible people too. Folks who messaged just to send love. No nosy questions. No trauma porn. Just care. 'Drop me a line when you're ready,' they said. Amidst all the trolls, half-baked takes and self-righteous conspiracy hunters, there were people—funny, thoughtful, deeply human. They cracked jokes laced with compassion, and I was the first to laugh.

One meme read: 'Sure, you've got problems but have you ever been middle-aged and scammed by a twenty-year-old?'

Another: 'Check on your middle-aged friends who made Gen Z besties.'

On the third day, I decided I had the strength to go for a walk. Sneakers on, hair tied into a wild bun, I stepped out. The streets felt familiar but surreal. I was wobbly, disoriented. And then my worst fear nearly ran me over.

A guy on a bicycle rolled towards me. I moved aside. He stopped. He seemed to be in his early twenties and was wearing joggers. I can't remember his face.

'Hey … you're Rheea, right?' he asked.

My heart stalled. My mouth filled with metaphorical jam.

'I saw your video.'

Misery of my own making. I had just wanted a fucking walk.

'It's crazy, right? How are you doing?'

'I'm still processing,' I croaked, nodding as subtly as possible, hoping he'd get the hint. Maybe he was a follower. My video had gone far beyond my modest 5K Instagram base. I didn't know him and yet I felt stripped, unsafe; even though, in hindsight, he probably meant well.

'So … are you going to file a police report?'

'Probably.'

He nodded. Approvingly? I couldn't tell.

'I'm going to take a walk now,' I said.

'Take care. All the best,' he said, pedalling off.

I kept my eyes on the pavement and walked briskly to the park. I walked round after round, no music, no podcast, just my brain doing its usual contortionist act.

Eventually, I got a lawyer. I filed the police report—sobbing, hiccupping, everything. I had to go back multiple times for follow-ups. One day, Phil and Mariam, friends who were online comrades, came with me for support. Their presence was a balm. Mariam gave me the number of a lawyer she trusted. For whole moments, I felt held.

I posted an update on Instagram, requesting privacy. There wasn't much more I could do. Unless people who donated wanted to file a civil suit, this wouldn't grow beyond a personal complaint.

I'd asked online if anyone wanted to join me in a civil case. No one did. But the moment I posted that I'd filed the FIR, people started asking: 'Why won't you share the FIR number?' My lawyer had said I couldn't. Bad-faith questions kept coming. I decided to go quiet.

So, what was happening inside me?

For a while, I did normal things. A family lunch at Filter Coffee in Indiranagar with my mom, my mother-in-law and Utsav. Sambar, palya, chutney, heaps of rice, papad. Then, my mom tried to herd everyone for a photo.

That's when it hit me.

I felt a *violent* fear of being captured on camera. A simple photo triggered dread. For someone who'd lived comfortably on Instagram, sharing selfies and bits of my every day, this was baffling. It had nothing to do with Sanch, not directly. But the idea of being 'seen' made me feel naked. Shameful. My mom understood instantly. I stepped out of the frame and took the photo instead.

Depression had always been my friend. But a betrayal of this magnitude didn't just deepen the ache, it lobotomized the parts already prone to spiralling. I'd never really dealt with anxiety, at least not in a way that felt diagnosable.

My psychiatrists over the years had settled on dysthymia: a long, low-grade depression and, occasionally, what they called 'double depression'. That's when chronic depression is punctuated by a heavier, more acute crash.

Most of my life had been lived under a steady hum of sadness. I could reach for bleakness and sustain it longer than I could joy. But my sassy mouth, my chaotic ambition, my ability to roast my loved ones into mushy laughter, that all kept me afloat. There was always a low ache under it all but I was high-functioning and hungry for life. Until I wasn't.

That's the 'double' in double depression. When Big D comes to visit depression lite. And when Big D shows up, the basics—brushing my teeth, taking a bath—become impossible tasks. I'd want to go on a walk but the thought of tying my laces would make my eyes well up.

Even in those moments, though, I could manage *something*: a deadline, a yoga video, a grocery list.

But the Sanch explosion, right at the start of 2024, metastasized. At first, it was panic I couldn't shake. I'd spent years building a mantra around integrity—'If your words are honest and your intent is clean, that's all you owe.' But the betrayal detonated that belief.

Suddenly, I didn't trust myself. The Rheea I'd spent my thirties building felt flawed, jagged, punctured.

Then came a heavy lethargy. Normally, in dark spells, I'd boot up the engine of dark-humoured resilience and push through. But this time, the engine was dead. Creativity felt stupid. The world's tragedies felt unreachable. I posted a few photos in February and March but when I looked at them later, all I saw were ghosts, one smiling, one posing, one trying to hold light in her eyes.

Then came anhedonia. A word I'd read before but never really *met*. Anhedonia isn't despair. It's worse. It's the absolute absence of feeling. Not joy, not sorrow, just numbness. I, who couldn't watch a cartoon animal die without sobbing, who gave spontaneous monologues about the tragic beauty of the human condition, I felt nothing.

No excitement over new shows. No relief from petting my dog. Utsav's gentle encouragements sounded like garbled radio static. I imagined dead flowers falling from the sky. I couldn't taste the world. Not even the bitter parts.

I know the nervous system. I've studied how trauma wires the body. I know how our instinctive stress responses—freeze, flight, fawn—form over time. Mine had always been freeze and flight. But now, I wasn't running or freezing. I was shut down. Offline. When I reread Charlotte Perkins Gilman's 'The Yellow Wallpaper', I felt an eerie kinship with the protagonist who unravelled under well-meaning cruelty.

Except my madness wasn't conjured by a husband. It was conjured by a twenty-year-old woman who understood the language of trauma so perfectly she could make wounds out of the words that were made to heal. My neurons had Sanch embedded in them like parasites. I'd shake my head violently, as if I could rattle her out of my brain.

And then came the suicidal thoughts.

Every day I thought about a knife. I imagined the cut, the blood, the pain. I imagined freedom. The body releasing the soul. A return.

That's when Utsav and I knew something had to change. Adjusting meds wasn't working.

I'd lost one of the great loves of my life to suicide in 2016. We'd briefly been together in 2007 but his death, which I found out through a Facebook post, broke something permanent in me. I'd never stopped believing I'd see him again. When he died, that thread of hope turned to ash.

Back then, I wrote an essay after reading about the early ketamine trials to treat depression. It was part eulogy, part speculative fiction. What if he'd had access to ketamine? What if it had given him one more hour, one more day?

I never thought I'd be the one signing a consent form for ketamine treatment.

Ketamine was developed in the 1960s as a dissociative anaesthetic which was safe, fast, effective, even in warzones.[1] In the early 2010s, research into its use for treatment-resistant depression gained steam. By 2019, it was mainstream in the US, even approved in nasal spray form by their Food and Drug Administration. It had a street identity too—it was known as Special K, or Vitamin K, and gave users a dreamy, dissociative high, depending on dose and context.

This wasn't woo-woo. It was science. And I was desperate enough to try it.

When I found a clinic thirty minutes from my home, it felt like the first flicker of real hope. Utsav said he'd support me 100 per cent. I was terrified. I'd never done hard drugs—I had barely smoked a joint or taken a Vicodin in college. Ketamine felt like a big deal.

The doctor was kind. Calm. A little philosophical, which I liked. He explained the science, the risks, the metaphysical angle of it all.

'You might see your own death,' he said. I nodded like I understood.

The clinic was immaculate. Clean. Expensive by Indian standards but nothing compared to US rates. I signed the forms. Utsav looked uneasy. I looked into his eyes, trying to convey, 'Thank you for being here, even if it scares you.'

A nurse took my vitals and asked if it was my first time. I nodded.

On the hospital bed was a pillow and a blanket. The room had a gently humming AC. The doctor added the dose to the IV.

'You'll start to fade in a few minutes,' he said.

Utsav sat beside me, two feet away, holding my hand. I felt a gentle heaviness. Then my tongue swelled up. I heard myself swallow. Then—

I left.

No body. No Earth. No concept of time. I was floating in something like space but not space. A dark, expansive nowhere. And I thought: *I'll never come back to that bed. I'll never be Rheea again. I'm just … out here now.*

In this space, Utsav wasn't a man, he was a light. A soul. I recognized him only by his energy.

At one point, I became the air conditioner. I can't explain it. I *was* the AC. Everything was me. The bed. The machine. The atoms.

Then the truth came, not spoken, not heard, just *known*: I was a soul. Not in metaphor. Not as a concept. I *was* a soul.

It was epistemological, not academic, not borrowed. My body and mind had reached the same conclusion and the truth was mine.

Eventually, the light shifted. Utsav returned to form. The doctor came in.

'She's strong,' the doctor told Utsav. 'Most people stay down another hour.'

I smiled weakly. I could barely stand. Every movement felt like I was dragging sandbags through mud. I was given another shot for nausea and told to sit, hydrate, then head home.

In the back of the auto we took to go home, with my head on his shoulder, Utsav told me he had asked Manjula, our housekeeper and cook, to make my favourite soya curry. I hadn't eaten in twelve hours.

The warm breeze, the honking cars, all felt like a lullaby.

'I didn't think I'd make it back,' I whispered. 'It was scary. But it was ...'

'You don't need to explain it now,' he said. 'Let's get you home.'

Once home, I ate like a hungover college kid. Gulped water. Collapsed into bed.

And slept.

~

When ketamine is used to treat depression, the standard protocol is six sessions within a couple of weeks. I spread mine over three-and a-half weeks, which, let's be honest, is peak neurodivergent energy. The infusions themselves weren't unpleasant—no nausea, no hallucinated demon babies. But afterwards? You feel like you were hit by a tranquilizer dart. Sleepy, disoriented, gently obliterated.

My saving grace, my eternal frenemy, is my attention deficit disorder (ADD). I'm usually up and about every day, flitting between tabs, existential dread and my fifth cup of coffee. So, having entire days swallowed by ketamine recovery felt like being benched from my own chaos. Too much.

The trick with ketamine is this: you have to know from the beginning that you'll come back. You're not lost. You're not broken. You are exactly as trustworthy and resourceful as your regular coffee order at Third Wave, just temporarily turned into an astral jellyfish that can jump black holes and splash into new planets.

Once I accepted that, the later sessions became liberating. I was a universe-jumping wanderer with a day pass. I wasn't just floating aimlessly; I could guide myself. It was like levelling up in a video game where you're both the player *and* the map.

Some people see terrifying things during their sessions: demons, mirrors of shame, childhood bedrooms with slightly off lighting. Others puke, cry, spiral. Me? I was mid-tier. No drama. No horror. Just your average dimension-hopping, star-dissolving, mildly philosophical light show.

A major moment hit during a session where I saw all existence as particles, tiny specks of sand, each reacting to one another. Some sand stirred others, some were still, some formed masses and swallowed smaller specks. I thought, *this is us. This is humanity*. Just globs of consciousness reacting to stimuli like love, violence, grief. The genocide in Palestine had been weighing on me for months and here it was, a representation of our collective apathy and tolerance for deep evil: globs colliding, suffering, stirring.

And then, something clicked. We are nanoparticles. Infinitesimal. And yet, the very reason we exist is to *experience*. To give the unknowable universe a point of view. That's it. That's the job. I, Rheea, was the entire cosmos condensed into this particular location: a middle-aged Indian woman with a chaotic brain, an internet presence and a tendency to cry at animal deaths in animated movies.

Nothing more. Nothing less.

And just like that, the suicidal thoughts dropped off a cliff. A part of my ego, some desperate narrative insisting I was failing at life, melted. I was vast. And I could see the vastness in others with equal reverence. It was the closest I've come to grace.

The next five months were shockingly stable. My world-view had been unhinged in the best way. I had touched a truth: we are both completely irrelevant *and* exceedingly precious. That's the cosmic joke. The trickster logic of an unknowable universe playing dress-up in carbon forms. If everything is possible, then *everything*, every version of reality, every being, every pain, every pleasure, must exist.

That snapped the binary of good and evil off its hinges. It rewired something. It gave me a spiritual scaffolding I hadn't even known I was still searching for.

But here's the thing about insight. It's never permanent.

No world-view stays glued together forever. That would break the laws of reality itself. We are temporary creatures.

Our minds are soup. The peaks, the clarity, the beauty, all of it recycles. All of it bends.

And when it came to the aftershocks of Sanch, I still had one final quake to survive.

Technically, things were going well in September 2024.

It had been seven months since the disaster. No one had managed to trace Sanch. The police had stopped looking, claiming my evidence wasn't enough to pursue the case further, which, honestly, didn't surprise me. Even with a mountain of receipts, they shrugged it off.

But I didn't care anymore. I wasn't going to chase a deviant ghost through legal bureaucracy. She wasn't going to give people their money back. She wasn't going to give me my sense of safety back. There would be no justice, just echoes.

Moonbird Creative was finally getting great clients and doing work that felt real and purposeful. We had a big writing workshop planned for mid-September, sponsored by one of our clients in Australia. We were excited. We had cupcakes ordered, worksheets printed and our favourite local venue, Atta Galatta, locked in.

The day before the workshop was perfectly normal. I reviewed the schedule. My cofounder double-checked the catering. Sahithi prepped her camera gear. We were calm. Ready.

Until sunset.

That's when panic bloomed. I dismissed it as pre-event nerves. But it kept growing. I started crying. It wasn't PMS,

I had just finished my period. It wasn't rational. It wasn't explainable.

In hindsight, building a business while healing from betrayal was brave. Doing ketamine therapy in the middle of all that? Radical. I'd even tried talk therapy again but my ADD brain had gotten bored after a few sessions. Everything I was doing, especially online, was loud, confident, funny, wholesome, edgy.

But showing up in real life? Teaching a real workshop? Maybe that's what cracked me open. Maybe my body remembered what my mind didn't want to admit: I was scared. Scared people would see through me. That I wasn't all that smart or stable or worthy. That I was stupid. Brash. Enabling. Dumb.

By 7 p.m., I was trying to breathe through it. Utsav was beside me, counting my breaths. I started howling. And then, I went still. Catatonic. The tears kept flowing but I couldn't move. Couldn't speak.

'I need help. I need help,' I whispered over and over, like a broken chant.

Utsav found a 24/7 psychiatric hospital called Sukoon, almost an hour away. He messaged Sahithi. Told them I had a breakdown and he was taking me to get help. They became event-cancelling ninjas, sent graceful apology emails, rearranged logistics and told me not to worry about a thing.

I felt like I'd failed them. The guilt pressed into my chest like a knife. Not emotional pain. Just a physical stab. Nothing else could register.

I clung to Utsav in the car, head buried in his chest. At the hospital, I barely spoke. A doctor asked questions. Utsav did most of the talking.

'I can't talk,' I managed to say.

They admitted me. Gave me a shot of lorazepam. Checked my bags. Took my meds. Assigned me a clean, calm room. Utsav was allowed to stay.

It didn't feel like a hospital. It felt like a quiet, kind hotel. I fell into the plush bed and slept.

In 2008, I had worked as a behavioural counsellor in a psychiatric hospital. I always found the patients fascinating—people whose humanity had been shredded or tested by systems, drugs, institutions or themselves. The nurses were paranoid about pyjama strings and tampon boxes. One once told me: 'A woman tried to kill herself by swallowing a tampon and pouring water down her throat. It expanded. She survived. But after that, tampons were banned.'

I spent time on Unit One, where most patients had schizophrenia. Some were highly intelligent, using chalk to write messages to aliens or inventing whole languages, complete with right grammar and syntax.

Mental illness, I came to understand, is often a portal to alternative realities. The real suffering begins when the world tries to crush those realities into 'normalcy'. I saw pain, yes. But I also saw persistence. Surreal, brilliant, dangerous persistence.

Now, I was one of them.

It didn't feel ironic. It felt inevitable.

To be on both sides of that line has given me a clearer view of humanity than almost anything else in my life. As a human, I want to go full manifesto mode and write about psychiatry, systems, stigma. But as a writer, I know that's not what this book is for.

I stayed at Sukoon for three days.

Nothing magical happened. No divine lightning bolt hit me. Just time. I got time to say I am not okay. I did art therapy. Physiotherapy. I talked to a psychiatrist who adjusted my meds. I got to lie down in the eye of my own storm and breathe.

And in that pause, I remembered the only truth that matters:

Just like I had traversed galaxies on ketamine, I could traverse this too. Whether it was a wormhole of hallucinated atoms or crash-landing in a psych ward, I had always found my way back. Even with a twenty-year-old shapeshifter who had burned down my life with the exact language I'd once used to survive it, I could still find a way.

CHAPTER 18

At the point of writing this book, I have not heard from Sanch since January 2024. She disappeared. I imagine her now as a spirit, once roaming Instagram fields, unveiling fragments of Silchar, Assam, Delhi, Bangalore, Mumbai through photos. Pieces of a life we thought we knew.

I can close my eyes and picture her: plump cheeks, keratin-infused hair, her signature serious-satire face. I can hear voice notes in her baby talk and see her stories, the ones that dared to declare she was a former sex worker. The ones that chose bold, aggressive typography to call out the latest 'grifter' influencer, usually a 'dumb cunt' who, in her words, needed to read some social theory before talking rot. I had admired her butcher-style bluntness, the zero-bullshit delivery, until I realized everything about her was bullshit.

Only the details of Sanch's story are unique. The archetype isn't. There are thousands of Sanchs, different faces, same anatomy. People who lack empathy and use that very deficit to wound others. People whose own mental distress gets alchemized into cruelty, deliberately making others feel smaller, stupider, less competent.

And my story? My spiritual 'insights' through this process? Not unique either. Many of us, bright-eyed, idealistic, foolishly fast to glorify the best in someone, create delusions of goodness where none exist. My reckoning mirrors those found on Reddit threads about near-death and out-of-body experiences. Lived experience matters, yes, but it rarely offers certainty or a singular truth. We mirror each other's truths. We reject the ones that don't resonate.

Power, I've realized, is something we all engage with. We tend to think of it as one person manipulating another, as calculated, cruel, coercive. And yes, that kind of power is vile and must be escaped. But power is often quieter, subtler.

It can be a well-meaning elder's advice. A spouse saying you look good only in white and peach. A reel that fills you with joy. A TV show whose dialogue lingers on your tongue for weeks. A book that detonates your world view and lives in your casual conversations thereafter.

You might say, 'Isn't that just influence?' I'd argue: power is what charms you into practice. It becomes influence only when you embody it. Not all control is bad. But if you're not aware of the power you choose to carry or, worse, the power being used on you, you'll never fully understand your own boundaries or values.

Everything we engage with exerts some level of control. Our job is to ask: is this helping me grow and learn? Become someone who recognizes that human history is a looping reel of the same stories told differently?

We're social animals. We evolved through community. A mother nurses another woman's child while she cooked for the tribe. We borrow sugar from neighbours. We lend our cycle to a college kid trying to get to class. We rally funds for someone evicted for being queer. We babysit, cook, clean, grieve, love. We ask someone to read our poems. We post our vulnerable art. We trust.

And in trusting, we build, recreate, reimagine.

I've asked myself, of course, what my transparency here offers you. Part of this book will resonate with those who have been betrayed. Someone like Sanch is not rare. She is replicable. Familiar. Predictable.

The other part is this: humans are ever-expanding patterns. When we're lucky, we catch flashes of each other's humanity. I've shared those flashes with so many—some gone, some still to come. This is essential. It's what lets us walk into new connections with the fragile hope that we'll be met with compassion, with mistakes, with repair.

Some people use words to sound well-read, immaculate, stunningly charming. Some possess none of that but live radical kindness every day. Some have both. But words are never enough. Identity politics is never enough. When wielded with no self-reflection, it becomes as toxic as the systems it claims to dismantle. Especially in the circus of Instagram. If you can't critique your own circle, if you can't hold yourself to the standards you expect of others, maybe shitposting is your highest calling.

I now understand why I was enraptured by Sanch. The power she held over me felt generative. Here was a young, aloof, intensely intelligent woman who had no fucks to give. In my twenties, I was ashamed, with two marriages blown up, years spent proving I could have a career, a writing life—one I fought for with endless rejection.

Sanch gave me permission not to be so hard on myself. To stop overexplaining. To let my takes fly. But I never needed her for that. I was always heading toward being blunt, flip, funny and deeply sensitive, all at once.

Now I know: Sanch is nothing. She was a mask. A brain full of SparkNotes summaries and a shameless liar. A girlboss grifter with no moral ballast, no reverence for the love people gave her.

Ankur texted me last week:

'Whenever Sanch feels lonely, empty, like she's drowning in the void, she will remember you, me and others like us who loved her. She'll know she'll never experience the one thing that counters all of it: being whole. Knowing she is incapable of filling the gaping hole in her heart. What a waste.'

Finally, what do we do with the memories? The grief for a friend who was never a friend? How do you make sense of mourning something that was fundamentally false?

Maybe it's not a question to answer. Maybe it's one we live.

The last anyone heard from Sanch was in a Reddit thread. Blurred photos. A new name. She was studying for 'general category' college exams, had found Jesus, had a boyfriend and was budgeting ₹10,000 for his birthday gift. Someone called her out. She deleted the thread. Vanished again.

She'll resurface. Sanch is the kind of woman who needs to be seen. They always do.

But my part of the story ends here.

She didn't change me. Not at my core. I won't let a ghost rewrite the code of who I am.

I will still trust. Still give. Still write big-hearted sentences. Still raise money when someone's in crisis. Still believe in the strange, beautiful mess of people. That's not naivety, it's a choice.

Because community isn't about perfect people. It's about knowing who to hold close, who to let go and who to call the hell out.

There will always be a Sanch. And no matter how wise you get, you can't always see them coming. But you do get faster at spotting the cracks. At trusting your gut. And when you can't, that's when you count on the people around you, those who come to you with no ego, no saviour complex, doing the quiet, necessary work of pointing out red flags so fewer people get burned.

And for now, I'm not here for purity or certainty. I'm here because of the cracked mirror I refused to throw away because, even in pieces, it keeps showing me who I am.

ACKNOWLEDGEMENTS

This book would not exist without the people who dragged me out of the emotional wreckage, poured metaphorical (and literal) tea into me and reminded me that the story, brutal as it was, had to be told.

First, to my partner, Utsav: you believed in me even in the months I could barely believe in myself. You were there, quietly, constantly, throwing life rafts my way with the patience of someone who knew I'd eventually grab one. I did. Thank you for being my home base.

Aparupa Gupta, thank you for being the first to help me spot the red flags and for sitting with me through each crucial moment, step by step, as I pieced the truth together. You've been a friend for over a decade and a survivor in ways that are real.

Sahithi Sirikonda, co-dreamer and co-builder of Moonbird, you make me believe that meaningful work, soft friendships and fierce accountability can coexist.

Nikhil Wadhwa, you were my comic relief, my digital bodyguard and the goofball who somehow gave me the fiercest kind of courage in the simplest ways.

Disha Chatterjee, my sister, my quiet cheerleader, the one who looked me dead in the eye and said, 'Please, you have to write this book now.' You gave me the push that mattered.

Shalini Rao, you gave me unconditional tenderness, the kind that sits quietly with you until you can breathe again. Vani Subramaniam, for the jokes, the bruises, the love and the lifelong ride-or-die contract I never signed but fully accept.

Manjiri Indurkar, you were the wise friend I needed in these messy matters—thank you for rapping my knuckles when I slipped and for always calling it like it is.

To my mum, Rosemary Mukherjee, who lovingly stood by me and took care of me during the depths of my depression.

Dr Abhijit Khandkar, for being a constant force of moral clarity and gentle action. Kalabati, for being an ineffable source of love and care throughout my adulthood, book or no book. @kc.vlaine, for being the most pragmatic and steady online presence during and after the scam and for helping me articulate the power dynamics in online spaces. I also have so much gratitude for @outcaste_vegans, for your heart, courage and commitment to the truth, both in your work and in our time of need.

To the wild hearts I met (or re-met) in 2025: Aleena, you've taught me that you can tell the truth, hold nuance and never weaponize it; instead, you use it to expand hearts.

Shaheen Peer, you showed me that new friendships can be steady, luminous, radically kind—and prone to spontaneous photoshoots.

Sukanya Borthakur, you've loved me through twenty different versions of myself over two decades. Thank you for choosing me every time.

Devrupa Rakshit, you proved that even our gossip-aunty selves carry wit and wisdom (and sometimes a little too much tea).

Kritika Datt, you live your values with fierce integrity and, yes, the cost is real—but so are the sweet, ripe fruits we get to taste from the seeds we dare to plant.

I must thank Manjula, who has cared for my home for more than a decade. The labour and love she brings each day make it possible for me to write, to work and to keep following the projects and passions that matter to me.

To Susanna George, who had my back with sharp legal clarity when I needed it most. To Philemon Thomas and Mariyam: thank you for the kindness and grounding you brought to this journey.

Kamna Singh, thank you for the trust, solidarity and truth we have shared and alchemized into courage.

To Jacaranda Literary Agency, thank you: Jayapriya Vasudevan, for believing in this story, and to Smita Khanna, my agent, for shepherding it with care. To Trisha Bora, my editor at HarperCollins India, thank you for championing this book from the very start, for seeing its multifaceted impact and for providing it with the editorial home it needed.

And to Ankur, there are no words big enough but I hope this book gets close.

To the therapists and doctors who were finally the right ones: thank you for reminding me that this, too, shall pass. It did. And sometimes it will again. The right help changes everything.

To the Instagram circles I love, full of contradictions, chaos and people who keep surprising me, you made me believe that connection, even in this pixelated era, is still real. Perhaps this will all fade into digital obscurity someday; maybe we'll meet again on some future app. But for this strange slice of time, it was the best of times, it was the worst of times.

Thank you for reading, for witnessing and for walking with me through this story.

NOTES

Chapter 4

1. https://bjs.ojp.gov/content/pub/pdf/fvs03.pdf?utm_source=chatgpt.com
2. Sunu C. Thomas, 'Childlessness and intimate partner violence in India: Evidence from the National Family Health Survey', Johns Hopkins Center for Global Women's Health & Gender Equity, https://publichealth.jhu.edu/sites/default/files/2025-04/CGWHGE-Sunu-Brief.pdf.
3. Wendy Wolfson, 'Study: Financial Abuse of Older Adults by Family Members More Common than Scams by Strangers', HSC News, University of Southern California, 15 August 2019, https://hscnews.usc.edu/study-financial-abuse-of-older-adults-by-family-members-more-common-than-scams-by-strangers.
4. Gemma Styles, 'The Rise of the Instagram Vegans', gemmastyles.com, 4 June 2016, https://www.gemmastyles.com/articles/the-rise-of-the-instagram-vegans.
5. https://www.veganfirst.com/article/vegan-first-and-vegplanet-join-hands-to-create-asias-largest-vegan-magazine
6. Rheea Rodrigues Mukherjee, 'Being Vegan and Anti-Caste: Why We Need to Hear from Marginalised Communities',

The News Minute, 19 September 2022, https://www.thenewsminute.com/voices/being-vegan-and-anti-caste-why-we-need-hear-marginalised-communities-168030.

7. Sylvia Karpagam, 'Whether One Is Casteist or Anti-Caste, Veganism Is Not a Solution', *The News Minute*, 7 October 2022, https://www.thenewsminute.com/voices/whether-one-casteist-or-anti-caste-veganism-not-solution-168675 .
8. Rheea Rodrigues Mukherjee, 'I Am Vegan but Veganism Is Arbitrary and Inconsistent', Medium, 17 May 2017, https://medium.com/@rheea/i-am-vegan-but-veganism-is-arbitrary-and-inconsistent-b4d8a6e3b581.

Chapter 9

1. David Marchese, 'What It's Like to Be a Sociopath', *The New York Times Magazine*, 23 February 2024, https://www.nytimes.com/interactive/2024/02/25/magazine/patric-gagne-interview.html.
2. 'History of PTSD and Trauma Diagnoses', Trauma Dissociation, https://traumadissociation.com/ptsd/history-of-post-traumatic-stress-disorder.html.
3. TED, 'Strange Answers to the Psychopath Test | Jon Ronson | TED', YouTube, 15 August 2012, https://www.youtube.com/watch?v=xYemnKEKx0c.
4. 'Speaking of Psychology: Recognizing a Narcissist, with Ramani Durvasula, PhD', Episode 37, *Speaking of Psychology*, American Psychological Association, 2016, https://www.apa.org/news/podcasts/speaking-of-psychology/narcissism.
5. https://www.youtube.com/@DoctorRamani
6. MedCircle, 'Narcissist, Psychopath, or Sociopath?', YouTube, 25 June 2018, https://www.youtube.com/watch?v=6dv8zJiggBs.

7. Elsa Ronningstam and Arielle R. Baskin-Sommers, 'Fear and Decision-Making in Narcissistic Personality Disorder—a Link between Psychoanalysis and Neuroscience', *Dialogues in Clinical Neuroscience* 15, no. 2 (1 April 2022): 191–202, https://pmc.ncbi.nlm.nih.gov/articles/PMC3811090/.
8. 'Abigail Marsh', https://abigailmarsh.com/.
9. Big Think, 'Why Altruism Is Selfish | Neuroscientist Abigail Marsh', YouTube, 13 September 2024, https://www.youtube.com/watch?v=sCf9z9uArO0.
10. RootsofEmpathy, 'Dr. Abigail Marsh - The Altruistic Brain', YouTube, 17 July 2019, https://www.youtube.com/watch?v=mxn_YuWDX1I.

Chapter 10

1. 'Gestalt Therapy', Psychology Today, https://www.psychologytoday.com/us/therapy-types/gestalt-therapy.

Chapter 15

2. Agnes Lindberg, 'Scam Alert: The Rise of the "FedEx Courier" Scam in India', Truecaller, 9 April 2024, https://www.truecaller.com/blog/scam-alert/scam-alert-the-rise-of-the-fedex-courier-scam.
3. The Brainwaves Video Anthology, 'Jennifer Freyd - Betrayal Trauma', YouTube, 19 August 2021, https://www.youtube.com/watch?v=PL1_IEDD2Hw.
4. https://www.youtube.com/watch?v=B4wl0cnmM10, https://www.youtube.com/@DoctorRamani

Chapter 17

1. Georges Mion, 'History of Anaesthesia: The Ketamine Story – Past, Present and Future', *European Journal of Anaesthesiology* 34, no. 9 (September 2017): 571–75, https://journals.lww.com/ejanaesthesiology/fulltext/2017/09000/history_of_anaesthesia__the_ketamine_story___past,.2.aspx.

ABOUT THE AUTHOR

Rheea Mukherjee is the author of *The Body Myth* (Unnamed Press & Penguin India, 2019), which was shortlisted for the Tata Literature Live! First Book Award, and *The Girl Who Kept Falling in Love* (Penguin India, 2023). Her books linger where desire, disillusionment and rebellion collide, charting the brutal, tender and often ridiculous ways we try to love, grieve and make sense of ourselves. Her work has appeared in the *Los Angeles Times*, BuzzFeed, Electric Literature, Scroll and *Southern Humanities Review*.

Raised in India and the US, Rheea writes from the uneasy intersections of place, memory and cultural expectation. Her diasporic lens is sharp, unsentimental and alive to the contradictions of Indian urban life while casting a critical glance at the brittle promises of the American Dream.

She currently co-runs Moonbird Creative, a creative communications studio in Bangalore. Rheea's public work focuses on mental health, justice and the small, stubborn rebellions that keep us human. You can follow her at @rheealization, where the stories continue, unfinished, curious and chaotic.

HarperCollins *Publishers* India

At HarperCollins India, we believe in telling the best stories and finding the widest readership for our books in every format possible. We started publishing in 1992; a great deal has changed since then, but what has remained constant is the passion with which our authors write their books, the love with which readers receive them, and the sheer joy and excitement that we as publishers feel in being a part of the publishing process.

Over the years, we've had the pleasure of publishing some of the finest writing from the subcontinent and around the world, including several award-winning titles and some of the biggest bestsellers in India's publishing history. But nothing has meant more to us than the fact that millions of people have read the books we published, and that somewhere, a book of ours might have made a difference.

As we look to the future, we go back to that one word—a word which has been a driving force for us all these years.

Read.

Harper Collins   Harper Sport   HARPER FICTION   HARPER NON-FICTION   हार्पर हिन्दी

HARPER LEARNING   HARPER VANTAGE   HCCB HARPERCOLLINS CHILDREN'S BOOKS   4th   HARPER PERENNIAL

HARPER DESIGN   BOOKTOPUS   HARPER BUSINESS